P

The Key Place

"In *The Key Place*, Gene Shelburne invites us into a century-old house in the dusty west Texas town of his ancestral roots. You will cross a threshold into a place pulsing with memories of the family it warmed and nurtured for half a century—not mere maudlin nostalgia, but towering memories of tenaciously held values that shaped generations to come. Enter and let Shelburne's vivid style and discerning insight take you into a past that will enlighten your future."

—**Thomas Williams**, bestselling author of fourteen books

"In *The Key Place*, Shelburne invites us to make a series of pilgrimages with him to a former home, where wit and personal recollections flow together, arousing the reader's own streams of reminiscence and prompting reflections on faith, wisdom, our changing culture, and lessons to be learned. With characteristic warmth and earnestness, the author transports us into colorful scenes rich with homespun texture where we find ourselves alternating between laughter and sober reflection. Mixing some wistfulness at the days gone by with thoughtful portents about the realities ahead, the book is consistently positive, finding many reasons for great hope as we step into God's future together. Against the backdrop of the old home place, this book is an affable companion in a journey of reflection on home as it was, is, and will be."

—**Jeff Childers,** Carmichael-Walling Professor of New Testament and Early Christianity; coauthor of *The Crux of the Matter* and *Unveiling Glory*

"Gene Shelburne is in the top tier of Christian writers. His prose is, in my opinion, equaled by few, surpassed by none. This gifted author's works never accumulate dust on my desk—they go to the top of my Read-Next pile. Poring over his words, I am always blessed—going to bed a wiser and better man than I was when I woke up. In this extraordinary book, Gene Shelburne adopts Jesus's model of teaching by parable— beginning each chapter with a story about his boyhood at *The Key Place*; then transporting us from his yesterday to our today with on-target application."

—**Dr. Joe Barnett,** minister, writer, publisher

"Realistic about life's traumas, yet full of hope and healing, and with a foundation of the Lord's power to redeem any situation and bring good from it, Gene Shelburne's writing has much to offer in today's hurting world."

—**Michael Phillips,** author and publisher

"Some authors tell their stories well, but few as well as Gene Shelburne. Through his finely tuned and well-crafted writing, you will be drawn inexplicably into his private world. Sit for a spell. Enjoy the warmth and hospitality of *The Key Place*. As you watch and listen to Gene's discovery of himself, you may also find yourself. Read it and reap!"

—**Mary Hollingsworth,** bestselling author and publisher

The Key Place

AN ORDINARY PLACE TO MEET
AN EXTRAORDINARY GOD

Gene Shelburne

LEAFWOOD
PUBLISHERS
an imprint of Abilene Christian University Press

THE KEY PLACE

An Ordinary Place to Meet an Extraordinary God

LEAFWOOD

P U B L I S H E R S

an imprint of Abilene Christian University Press

Copyright © 2015 by Gene Shelburne

978-0-89112-606-5 | LCCN 2015004750

Printed in the United States of America

Scripture quotations, unless otherwise noted, are from The Holy Bible, New International Version®, NIV®. Copyright © 1973, 1978, 1984 by Biblica, Inc.® Used by permission. All rights reserved worldwide.

Scripture quotations noted KJV are taken from the King James Version of the Bible.

Scripture quotations noted RSV are taken from the Revised Standard Version of the Bible, copyright 1952 [2nd edition, 1971] by the Division of Christian Education of the National Council of the Churches of Christ in the United States of America. Used by permission. All rights reserved.

Scripture quotations noted NASB are taken from the New American Standard Bible® Copyright © 1960, 1962, 1963, 1968, 1971, 1972, 1973, 1975, 1977, 1995 by The Lockman Foundation. Used by permission.

Scripture quotations noted NRSV are taken from the New Revised Standard Version Bible, copyright © 1989, the Division of Christian Education of the National Council of the Churches of Christ in the United States of America. Used by permission. All rights reserved.

Scripture quotations noted *The Message* taken from *The Message*. Copyright 1993, 1994, 1995, 1996, 2000, 2001, 2002. Used by permission of NavPress Publishing Group.

LIBRARY OF CONGRESS CATALOGING-IN-PUBLICATION DATA
Shelburne, Gene, 1939-
  The key place : an ordinary place to meet with an extraordinary God / Gene Shelburne.
     pages cm
  ISBN 978-0-89112-606-5
  1. Meditations. I. Title.
  BV4832.3.S49 2015
  242--dc23
                                                                                    2015004750

Back cover photo courtesy of: Library of Congress, Prints & Photographs Division, OR-129-D

Cover design by Kent Jensen
Interior text design by Sandy Armstrong, Strong Design

Leafwood Publishers is an imprint of Abilene Christian University Press
ACU Box 29138, Abilene, Texas 79699

1-877-816-4455 | www.leafwoodpublishers.com

                    15 16 17 18 19 20 / 7 6 5 4 3 2 1

To my brothers—all three of them—
who treasure our heritage at the Key Place as much as I do.

Acknowledgments

When the critical mass of the writing in these pages began to reach potential book size, I dumped an early stage of the manuscript on the desk of my lifelong friend and first-line editor, Tom Williams. For years Tom has been one of the top professionals in religious book writing and publishing. His early input on this one was invaluable.

Leonard Allen blessed me years ago by sticking out his neck to publish my book, *The Quest for Unity*. What a grand surprise he gave me when, just before he took off his Leafwood hat, he called to tell me that he was putting this manuscript onto Leafwood's publishing calendar for the coming year.

My own book-editing labors for Leafwood have been more than repaid as Gary Myers, Duane Anderson, Mary Hardegree, Frank Steele, and other Leafwood staffers have toiled to polish this manuscript and to market the final product.

To adequately thank all the people who contribute to any published work obviously is impossible. But I would be remiss if I failed to tip my hat to all the neighbors and Coke County characters who have made my days in the dusty little town of Robert Lee, Texas, worth writing about.

Table of Contents

Preface

Several times a year—not nearly often enough—my brothers and I slip away from the hectic world we live in to hide away with books and laptops at our Key grandparents' old home in the small West Texas town of Robert Lee.

Shortly before supper Tuesday evening, I rolled up onto the elevated gravel drive and parked my burgundy PT Cruiser just outside the front gate in the space reserved for Granddaddy's cattle truck all the years I was a boy. I killed the engine and sat there for a moment, just savoring the feeling of being "home" again. I don't think I was exaggerating when later that evening in an email to a friend I confided, "This is my favorite place on God's green earth."

Not many hours earlier—right before I loaded my bedroll and my study materials into my car to head south—a colleague expressed some surprise that I would elect to drive almost three hundred miles each way to find a quiet place to study and write. "Wouldn't you be more productive if you found some quiet place nearer to town and used those hours on the road to work instead of to drive?"

I tried to explain to him that the drive seems to be part of the magic in my retreats to this place. When Nita and I used to enjoy weekend retreats at Laity Lodge, I told my friend, for the last quarter mile of our journey to the lodge we literally drove in the water of the Frio River, using its flat rock bottom as our road. Somehow driving off dry land into that river provided us a kind of psychological disconnect with the stressed-out world we needed to escape. Once we drove up the gravel road out of the riverbed, we found ourselves in a rare world with no watches, telephones, televisions, or radios. For three magical days we left behind all of the day-to-day demands on the other side of that river. The physical separation was refreshing to our souls.

My wife and I enjoy vacationing in Victoria, B.C., partially for the same reason. When we drive onto the ferry and it pulls away from the mainland, we unconsciously but tangibly relax and turn loose of any concerns on the shore behind us. Days later when the homebound ferry disgorges us back on home soil, we resume our responsible roles in the real world. That ferry ride provides an effective buffer between the universe we normally labor in and the fairy-tale world of Victoria's Inner Harbour. The hours on the boat are part of the magic.

The four-and-a-half-hour drive from Amarillo south to Robert Lee does something like that for me. When I top the cedar-covered escarpment south of Silver and spot the buzzards circling in the thermals high above the rugged terrain on the west edge of Coke County, I know I have temporarily left behind what somebody aptly called the "tyranny of the urgent." I have dropped out of a world where too many people know my phone number and too many have somehow managed to get their name inscribed on a slot in my calendar. As I coast past ranch land that borders the vanishing lake just west of town, I know that I have temporarily escaped the spate of pastoral demands that virtually stifle any possibility of creative thinking and writing. In my heart I give thanks that the hours just ahead will be all mine.

I understand why Moses kept going back to that mountain.

I know why Jesus needed forty days alone in the desert.

It took Saul three years of solitude in Arabia before Jesus got that fanatic's heart and head straight. Why should it surprise anybody that I often yearn for more than three days to be alone here with the Lord and to listen for the whisperings of his Spirit?

That is part of the answer to my friend's query about my choice to come so far to this tiny old house in a vanishing village. But there is so much more. I doubt that a single volume can contain enough pages for me to tell it all to you, so, hopefully, others may follow this one.

In the series she called *The Crosswicks Journal*, that marvelous writer and teacher of writers, Madeleine L'Engle, filled four truth-laden volumes in her attempt to explain the complex impact her visits to her much-loved home in Crosswicks had on her faith and her family relationships and her prolific creative output. I'm not sure she ever got it fully told, but in the effort to do so, that remarkable lady traces the outlines of a spiritual journey, and the telling has blessed countless souls. When she tells how living in that Crosswicks farmhouse touched every facet of her life and shaped every fiber of her soul, I read her words and nod with comprehension. The Key Place has done the same for me.

As my Key Place reflections have sprangled from a few isolated anecdotes into a more complex web of multigenerational memories, I have begun to perceive that something deeper still may drive my yen to roost on what has become for me and my brothers an almost sacred piece of ground.

I suspect that God built into each of us a homing instinct, not unlike the drive that causes a salmon in the Pacific more than three thousand miles from its birthplace to head north, navigating unerringly to the headwaters of some tiny Alaskan stream. When that mighty fish gets there, she knows she is home. She has found the one place on earth—the key place—where she belongs.

Time was when humans lived and died within a few miles of where they were born. It was a simpler time, and perhaps a healthier one. And even those roamers like Vasco da Gama and Christopher Columbus never rested until they had completed the round trip and were once more back home.

One aged fellow I met in Arkansas told me rather proudly that he had never once in his life ventured outside of his county. He knew his place on earth, and he was quite content to stay there. Before the advent of sails and steam engines and internal combustion motors, that old fellow's tale would not likely have been all that unusual. The majority of people on earth lived and died within eyeshot of the same terrain. Could it be that in this age of modern nomads, when members of the same family often live and work on separate continents, we yearn even more intensely for the key place we call home?

Even for those of us who stay closer to our roots, our habits seem to confirm that something within us homes in on key places where we can be ourselves, where we feel free from external pressures, where we can connect with our inner selves and with the God our busyness tends to keep at bay.

Like neighborhood dogs, most of us identify those places where we feel most comfortable and secure, and we "mark" them as ours.

One of the dear widows in my church embarrassed us a few years ago. "You can't sit there. That's my pew," she informed an unsuspecting couple who had come to visit our worship that morning. It wasn't. Not really. But she had worshipped in that same spot for so many Sundays in a row that she couldn't imagine sitting anywhere else. She didn't mean to be rude or unfriendly to the squatters who mindlessly invaded her turf. She just wanted "her" spot on "her" pew.

Do you have a favorite chair where you read or watch TV? I do. And my wife also has hers. It's not that we mean to be selfish or touchy. We're just humans, and by nature we are territorial. At your family's breakfast table, does each member know who sits where? We do at my house. And, if we migrate to an unfamiliar place like a vacation condo, each of us finds his or her spot at the new table by the second or third meal. Nobody has to assign us a chair. Each of us soon knows where to sit. We know our place.

Once a month half a dozen of my colleagues and friends gather before dawn to share breakfast at Calico County restaurant. We always sit at the same table—*our* table. On the rare occasions when someone beats us to it, all of us feel a bit awkward and out of place. We try to be nice about it, but on those mornings when we get rearranged, breakfast just doesn't taste as good. The morning's visit doesn't go as well. Because we sense that we're not where we belong.

This homing instinct seems to work both on the macro and micro levels. We humans establish comfort zones both in kitchens and on continents. Henry David Thoreau had his Walden Pond. Eisenhower had his Camp David. Shakespeare's roots were in Stratford-on-Avon. The list could go on endlessly. All of us seem to have our key places.

Perhaps this explains the universality of Naboth's sad tale. When the king cast covetous eyes on that good man's vineyard, Naboth had no intention of selling it. Even if wicked Ahab had quadrupled the market price for that piece of land, Naboth's answer to his offers would still have been No. That vineyard had been tilled by his father, and by his grandfather before him. Every vine, every hedgerow, every terrace bore the stamp of Naboth's clan. Only the slope of that particular terrain suited his soul. Only the shade of those familiar trees comforted his body. As long as he had breath in his lungs, Naboth intended to hang on to that cherished piece of land.

Except for the treacherous way the king stole that vineyard, Naboth's story sounds like a carbon copy of the Chicago folks who were about to be plowed under by the projected expansions of O'Hare Field. No amount of money could erase their ties to ancestral real estate. "We don't care if the price we're being offered will let us live out our lives in luxury," they told the judge. "We want to spend the rest of our days on our property."

You know how the story of Naboth ended, of course. His link to his family acreage was so strong that he was willing to die before giving it up. That's how important the bond tends to be between most of us and the key places in our lives.

If this were just my story—just a part of my own clan's lore— both you and I would be wise to wonder if it's worth my time or yours to rehearse it. But the postmodernists have got at least this much right: *truth resides primarily in stories.* As one talented storyteller puts it, the truth is in the particulars.

God recognized this when he set out to show us his divine purposes and plans for saving our world. Instead of giving us a library of abstract soteriological theories and anthropological studies of sweeping racial migrations, the Creator of heaven and earth chose instead to tell us the true story of one nomadic sheepherder's trek from Iraq to Israel.

With surprising specificity, God told us not only the names of Abraham and his wives (all three of them), but he went on to list his kids and grandkids. In holy Scripture the Lord saw fit to define eternal salvation by telling us tales about the domestic upheavals in that old man's family, tales Abraham probably didn't care to have published for you and me and the rest of the world to see. By telling real stories with surprising attention paid to the particulars, God put into Paul's grasp everything the apostle would need to explain in Romans 4 how God's children today can be justified by faith.

I want to tell you some true stories about real people (my people) in a real place (the Key Place). Not because I think my people are in any way more special than yours. But because I am convinced that in the specifics of our stories you will discover your own. In our struggles to know God and to discern his will, I believe you will identify the turmoil of your own soul. Our tears will almost certainly turn out to be your tears, our failures your failures, our joy your joy.

Chapter 1

The Floor beneath the Floor

When I bought the Key Place from my ailing grandparents, I really could not afford to do so. But I was determined to find a way.

Word got out among the relatives that my mother and her siblings were emptying the old house, getting ready to put it on the market. Various relatives carted off knickknacks, pictures, dishes, and items of furniture, most of it worthless to anybody but those of us who had heartstrings tied to those pieces of junk.

No longer able to live alone safely in the home they had built before the Depression, my grandparents had migrated three blocks east to live in a tiny bedroom at my Aunt Vernie's place. They took with them a few odds and ends—a chair, a chest, a few pictures, and their sparse collection of clothing—just those possessions necessary to exist, since space in their new place was so limited.

When the sorting and parceling out of the remaining possessions was complete, my grandparents' kids swept out their old home and hauled the trash to the creek bank, leaving behind a starkly empty, cold, lifeless house where for so many years laughter and love and labor had abounded.

Almost three hundred miles away in the Texas Panhandle, I got word that my Uncle David thought he had the house sold. Everything within me screamed No. He and his sisters had concluded realistically that the family had no further use for the house they had grown up in. Keeping the residence with its acreage any longer could only be a needless expense—a senseless burden—with upkeep, taxes, insurance, and all the costs that go with owning property. Once their decision was made, they cried a few tears and got on with the business of selling their childhood home.

"I'm not sure what I can do," I told my uncle on the telephone that day in 1974. "I may not be able to afford it, but if you get an offer on the place, please call me and give me a chance to match it." I just could not imagine not having access to the pens and pecan trees and sheds and creek bed that had been my personal haunt all my days.

Much sooner than I expected, my uncle called. "I'm talking to a local fellow who wants to buy Mom's and Dad's property," he told me. The price they had negotiated was reasonable, but for me at that moment I knew it would be a stretch.

"Let me visit with my banker this afternoon," I requested. "I'll get back to you no later than tomorrow morning."

Noel Bruce was not just my banker. He was also my friend. Already he had underwritten my foray into the world of dilapidated rental houses, so he knew I probably owed him as much as I should. But I think Noel sensed that my request for funds to purchase the Key Place was not just another investment. This deal was tied not nearly so much to my head as to my heart, and my friend saw this. I left his office that afternoon with every dollar I needed to make the deal.

I tell you all of this to explain that during those first years after my grandparents' place became mine, I had little choice. I had to rent the house to pay for it. During the seven years it took me to retire that bank note, my brothers and I had little access to the house. For all but a month or two of that time, somebody we hardly knew lived in it. And, as so often is true for lower-rent property, our tenants were often not kind to the house and surrounding grounds.

One family brought along a couple of horses, penning them inside fences that were constructed primarily for sheep or goats. Months later when I showed up to inspect the place, half of our wire fences were sagging or totally wiped out—flattened by horses leaning across them to munch on the farthest possible sprig of grass, which, as everybody knows, is always greener on the other side. Some of those fences are still missing or drooping four decades later.

By far the worst damage, however, occurred inside the old house, hidden from our cursory inspections when we occasionally drove past on the street. I recall one Hispanic family who rented the place for about a year and a half. For the most part, they took good care of the property. They were decent folks, but the language barrier made communication a hassle, so they would go far too long without notifying us about minor plumbing problems we would have fixed. When they moved out, I found extensive water damage where their washing machine had leaked for months on the kitchen floor.

"I need to run over to Robert Lee one afternoon this week," I told Portis Ribble, my friend and colleague, when I showed up at his San Angelo church to work alongside him for several days right after those renters had told us *adios.* There I was that week, just thirty miles from my property instead of the usual three hundred, and if at all possible while attending to my preaching duties in San Angelo, I needed to grab some hours to go repair that water-buckled floor. Already I had new tenants who wanted to move in their belongings.

"No problem," Portis responded. And then he volunteered, "I'll go with you." So on that Thursday afternoon we traded our preaching garments for carpenter togs and headed north, not quite sure what that afternoon's task might entail.

Evidently my tenant's washing machine had leaked enough to keep the floor under it saturated. In the spot where it had stood near the back wall of the kitchen, the tiles had popped up and the wooden floor was visibly buckled. Obviously this portion of the floor would have to be replaced. To do this, I needed to know which way the joists ran beneath the flooring, but that was easier said than done. The house had been built before indoor plumbing or central heating came to West Texas. With no plumbing lines under the structure, the original builder had seen no reason to provide any crawl space. Nobody in my generation had ever peeked beneath that floor.

Portis and I stood and scratched our heads as we wondered how to attack the job at hand. "Before we start sawing big chunks of wood," I suggested, "let's drill a hole right here where the damage is worst. Then we can saber-saw a hole big enough for us to see the joists and plan for more precise cuts outside this water-soaked area." He agreed with my strategy, so I inserted the largest bit my trusty old drill would hold and bored a hole in the floor. The depth of the wood surprised me.

"Must have a layer of subflooring under the top boards," I surmised, still assuming that our eventual cuts would reveal at least a top layer of traditional half-inch-thick tongue-and-groove oak flooring.

With the longest saber-saw blade in my box, I soon cut out a circle about three inches across. When that donut of wood broke loose and fell through to the ground below, what I saw amazed me. The sides of the fresh-cut hole revealed that the original flooring in the house was made up of beautiful, solid oak boards about an inch and a quarter thick. I had never seen anything like it.

We later discovered that those massive boards had no set width. They ranged anywhere from five inches to fourteen inches wide. Shipped in the 1920s on a mule-drawn wagon from a sawmill near Brownwood, about a hundred miles to the east, the boards had been trimmed to whatever width each tree would allow. Few modern carpenters have ever known the thrill of working with fine wood of that size and quality.

Atop that solid, almost indestructible floor, my grandfather had glued on linoleum—the ancient kind—not nearly as tough or resilient as our modern flooring products. By the time World War II was over and the number of in-laws and grandkids had mushroomed, the surface of that first linoleum had been scuffed off, leaving ugly black splotches in the heavy traffic areas. I had forgotten that faded, defaced linoleum, but when we uncovered a swatch of it that day, faint childhood memories surfaced and I recalled that old floor with its marred surface showing the wear of almost twenty years of family footsteps by the time I was a boy.

I had also forgotten how my grandfather decided to repair that worn-out linoleum. Instead of scraping it off the oak floor, he took the easy route advised by a floor tile salesman. They tacked a layer of quarter-inch plywood right on top of the linoleum, thus providing a fresh, clean, smooth surface for the new tile. My exploration hole cut through all those layers and became a sort of archaeological dig, exposing the various stages from the distant past to the present.

As I knelt there and looked at the telltale strata in the floor, I was a bit sick to think I had just cut a hole in that exquisite oak flooring. Instantly it was obvious to Portis and me that the water damage we wanted to repair had affected only the plywood layer on the top. The damage was only skin deep. Months of moisture had loosened the tiles and caused the plywood to disintegrate and bubble up, but the original linoleum had protected that marvelous layer of oak beneath it. It was dry, flat, in pristine condition—just as solid as the day in 1928 when it was first nailed in place.

Our job that day turned out to be much easier than I had anticipated. Quickly Portis and I cut out and replaced the rectangle of damaged plywood, covered the new plywood with a garish slab of modern linoleum that never came close to matching the existing tile, and, like another evangelist so many centuries ago, we "went on our way rejoicing."

I look back now and find it hard to believe that I had been in and out of the Key house all the days of my life without knowing how uniquely valuable its floor was. As a toddler, I had skipped and jumped and rolled and tumbled on that floor. Many a night I had slept on it on a pallet or—better yet—on a feather mattress. We cousins played jacks and Old Maid and toy trucks and Tinker Toys on that same floor. We sat on it while we pored through Sears and Roebuck catalogs—minus the lingerie pages, which had been discreetly removed by our grandmother.

On that same floor, we kids had clustered dozens of times to listen as Grandmother told us the exciting stories of heroes in the Bible. When we were little guys, the floor of that house was our racetrack, as half a dozen of us flew through the front door and out the back, playing cowboys and Indians or cops and robbers or kick the can, as the mood of the day dictated.

But, despite all the golden hours I spent on that floor, not once while I was growing up did I suspect that beneath the linoleum and later the asphalt tile laid hidden that vintage oak, so sturdy and flawless.

Real value is like that. Often it tends to hide. Perhaps because God designed his world to work that way. When he sent humanity the priceless message of salvation in his Son, in his divine wisdom, God packaged that treasure "in earthen vessels" (2 Cor. 4:7 KJV). When he created women, he made them so that their true beauty would reside not in expensive clothes or showy jewelry but in their "inner self, the unfading beauty of a gentle and quiet spirit" (1 Pet. 3:4–5).

When God sneaked onto our planet in human disguise, he used the same strategy. The prophet Isaiah in his famous 53rd chapter predicted that nothing about Jesus would be attractive or beautiful. The Gospels confirm this, telling us he was born into a peasant family who lived in a disdained community. It was just as Isaiah foretold, "As one from whom men hide their faces, we esteemed him not" (v. 3).

God put together his world in such a way that true value seldom presents itself in the spectacular or the ostentatious. Gold and silver lie hidden deep under scraggly terrain. He hid diamonds in gravel piles and emeralds in worthless clay. So why should it surprise us that he constructed his church the same way? "Not many of you were wise by human standards; not many were influential; not many were of noble birth," the apostle Paul reminded his converts. "But God chose the foolish things of the world to shame the wise; God chose the weak things of the world to shame the strong. He chose the lowly things of this world and the despised things—and the things that are not—to nullify the things that are" (1 Cor. 1:26–29).

Like that priceless oak wood hidden in those Key Place floors, God often conceals the best, the holiest, the most faithful people in his world, saving them as ordinary, everyday, simple members of unpretentious congregations. It is his favorite trick to play on people who use the world's yardstick to measure greatness.

Last night in our small church, we watched a DVD presentation by one of America's best-known, highly successful pastors. Successful, at least, if you measure success by how big his congregation is, how many people are on his staff, how many books he sold last year, or how many people in America know his name.

From all I know about him, I am convinced that this pastor is an upright man with a good heart full of genuine love for Jesus, so I do not intend my remarks here to disparage him or to discount the truth of his message. But, I must confess to you, I am a sucker for small congregations, and this famous fellow is an apostle for the megachurch, so on many matters his perspective and mine are worlds apart.

At the beginning of his highly listenable and well-presented lesson last night, this eloquent preacher reeled off several verses of Scripture to show that Jesus was often surrounded by crowds so big they were hard to control. And, wrenching a text or two to make them fit his premise, this man implied that anybody involved in valid ministry today would also be attracting large crowds.

In my heart I wanted to say, "Wait just a minute, my dear brother. Do you not remember what Jesus said about honoring us with his approval and presence when only two or three believers gather together? Do you not recall his warning that the *big* crowd would go down a broad road to destruction, while those who found the true and narrow path would be *few?* Have you not read the apostle Paul's repeated greetings to congregations that met in some Christian's home?"

I wanted to remind this articulate but disembodied pastor on our projection screen that nothing flamboyant or splashy shows up in the most common biblical descriptions of the church at work in the real world. In fact, Paul said the churches he planted and served were usually the opposite. He was himself content to be seen as a "fool for Christ's sake," and his congregations tended to be made up of handfuls of peasants and slaves and ragamuffins with dubious pasts (1 Cor. 4:10; 6:9–11). Why? Because God meant for his church to be like that. He "chose what is foolish in the world to shame the wise."

Dare we trade our Lord's embarrassing standards for those that make us feel more respectable in our neighbor's eyes?

Small churches are my passion—so much so that the big-church pastor I have just criticized would probably find me to be as off-center in my obsession as he is in his megachurch mentality. Could it be that he simply has not enjoyed as many blessed ministry opportunities in superb small churches as I have through the years?

How much poorer my life would be if I had never been invited to preach to the tiny rural church in the vanishing community of Lena, Indiana. God made no better people than these stalwart souls who for multiple generations have been the salt of the earth and the light of the world in that corner of Hoosier country.

Gerald and Ellen Thomas operated the only store in Lena. They sold eggs, meat, butter, bread, mouse traps, Mason jars, gasoline, and an amazing array of household supplies to their neighbors. But folks who dropped by the Thomases' store often came not so much to buy coffee or beans as to run some knotty problem by Gerald, who was seldom too busy to lend an ear and to offer a wise word of counsel.

Others, down on their luck, knew the Thomases would never let their kids go hungry. Only God knows how many people still had groceries on the tab when Gerald and Ellen finally bowed to health and age and shuttered their aging store. For almost half a century, they had dispensed a mixture of mercantile goods and mercy across the same counter while faithfully leading the Lord's people in that vibrant but slowly shrinking church in tiny Lena.

What if this godly couple, so keen to serve the Lord as effectively as possible, had decided to strengthen their discipleship by moving to the big city and joining a "successful" church? Surely such a move would have diminished, and not enhanced, their godly influence and their opportunities to serve God's people.

Blinded by our current obsession with bigness, however, we might be tempted to overlook or minimize this kind of quiet, modest ministry. We might fail to see the precious oak flooring in what appears to be a shabby house.

Like small churches, some individuals are good at hiding their true worth. David Redding tells about a fellow like that. I first met Dave face to face at a weekend retreat at Laity Lodge in the late 1970s, but I became acquainted with him years before that when a religious book club sent me a copy of his marvelous little book, *God Is Up to Something*. That book title pretty well sums up this extraordinary pastor's outlook on life. He is convinced that God is always up to something—often in ways we least expect. From Dave's prolific pen followed many more books, equally well-crafted—books that have blessed my soul.

Nita and I were attending a later Laity Lodge retreat when David Redding told us about his discovery of a unique West Texas cowboy he identified to us simply by the name Hondo. This crusty old cowpuncher resided an hour or so northeast of Laity Lodge, up in what Texans call the Hill Country, near a place Willie Nelson would later make famous: the little German community of Luckenbach.

Since David pastored a busy Presbyterian church in Ohio, the chances that he would ever cross trails in central Texas with a galoot like Hondo were infinitesimal. It's a cinch that Hondo would never have shown up voluntarily to instigate such a friendship. Had he known a preacher was in the county, he would have scurried to the north forty and laid low until such a scurrilous character cleared out of the territory.

Guys like Hondo are allergic to clergymen. And from what Dave told some of us about that old coot, Hondo was pretty good at keeping them at a distance. To say that his vocabulary was colorful would be a gross understatement. It was indigo blue. He couldn't discuss the sunrise or tell you the time of day without three pro-fanities and half a dozen irreverent allusions to deity. Dave said the first time he met Hondo, the nonstop stream of obscenities flowing from this wiry stranger's mouth almost wilted Dave's preacher-soul. He couldn't wait to get away from it.

But—if I remember correctly—Hondo's daughter became David Redding's friend, and David agreed to be her writing mentor. If Dave was going to help her, he had no choice but to endure occa-sional doses of her raunchy father. After the first shock of Hondo's verbal assault wore off, the pastor in Dave began to see more deeply into the heart of his unlikely new friend. And the closer he looked, the more he liked what he saw—so much so that eventually he wrote the preface for *Hondo*, the book Hondo's talented daughter wrote about her rough-hewn dad.

"When I stopped judging the man," Dave told us, "suddenly from the mouth of that colorful character I began to hear home-spun wisdom, enchanting tales, and almost poetic descriptions of the rugged world Hondo inhabited." He had managed to get past the rough exterior to discover the priceless oak beneath it all.

I suspect that all of us have some Hondos in our lives. My own Grandfather Key, the man who built this little house that still bears his name, was a lot like Hondo. He also was a rancher who was more comfortable around rattlesnakes and prickly pears and all manner of horned critters than around most people. He was a man of few words. While others blustered, he listened. While they volunteered simplistic answers to complex problems, he listened. While the people around him carped or caviled or commented or complained, he listened. Most of the time. And when he finally did open his mouth, the few words he spoke were filled with wisdom and good sense that would bless you if you were able to get past the *hells* and *damns* and similar expressions that always punctuated his speech.

The fact that his oldest daughter married a rather stiff preacher who often sat at his dinner table never did alter my grandfather's word choice. Not one iota. When four of his grandsons went into ministry, I couldn't tell that the multiplication of ministers under the Key roof made one whit of difference in our grandfather's vocabulary. The words he used to address his sheep and goats and bulls and heifers—which he loved with all his heart—seemed to him to be perfectly suitable for humans too.

I suppose this seeming crudeness would have been offensive to those who did not know that D. P. Key was the most honest man in the county. His was not the company-manners kind of morality all too common in polite society today. American theologian Reinhold Niebuhr was right when he said that the moral posture of too many people resembles a giraffe, "tall in the front but low in the rear." Not so my grandfather. His language might not fit in Sunday school, but when he told you something, you could count on its being true. If he promised you anything, it was as good as done. In the sense that Jesus meant it, my grandfather's yes was yes, and his no was no—unlike some of the folks at church, whose pure lips never uttered so much as a euphemized swear word, but who seemed to be seriously truth-challenged when they promised to pay their bills or to be true to their mates.

None of the rest of us in the family dared to borrow Granddaddy Key's vocabulary on a regular basis, but his cowpuncher lingo somehow seemed okay coming from his mouth, because not once in all the years we knew him did we ever hear anything hateful or ugly or angry come out of his mouth. We knew how much he loved us, how much he respected his neighbors, how gently and fairly he dealt with all men. Somehow his heart seemed to make up for his expletives. Beneath the veneer, we knew the truly good man inside. At the core we had seen honest-to-goodness oak.

Do you remember when Michael Phillips reintroduced George MacDonald's great stories to American readers? He made those grand tales accessible to a new generation in a different world by paraphrasing the opaque Scottish brogue and minimizing the extensive preaching in the tales told by that extraordinary pastor-turned-novelist. In the volume Phillips retitled as *The Shepherd's Castle,* MacDonald describes his main character, Donal, as a man "who never loved wisdom so much as when she appeared in peasant garb" (22). MacDonald meant that as a compliment—a plus in his hero's character. Donal would have liked Hondo. He would have welcomed my Grandfather Key as a wise man.

Not all of us are blessed with that clarity of insight. We are too easily beguiled by the pedantry of academic credentialing and the specious trappings of sophistication. We mistake smoothness for competence, pomposity for substance. So we have only ourselves to blame when we are duped by charlatans whose only claim to our attention lies in their ability to make us feel dumber and less qualified than they are.

Outside his kingdom, Jesus told his men, are those who feign greatness by "lording it over" others. But true greatness, Jesus said, belongs only to those who will humble themselves as children, those who will accept the menial role of a slave. The way up is down, Jesus tells us. "He who humbles himself will be exalted." Christ's original Twelve at first seemed unable to absorb this lesson. They kept lobbying for positions of honor and power in his kingdom, while, as Anglican theologian Robert Farrar Capon puts it so memorably, Jesus tried to teach his men to discern true worth in "the last, the least, the lost, the little, and the dead" (*The Parables of Grace* 127).

This still seems to be the one truth most likely to elude our Lord's followers. Sheldon Vanauken writes in *A Severe Mercy* about approaching God through "high" or "low" doors. We need to listen when he assures us that the "low door probably leads to a throne" (152).

Today as people in Robert Lee walk or drive down our street, if they pay any attention at all to the Key Place, all they likely see is an unimpressive abode—better maintained than some of the older places nearby, for sure—but still a house that cannot hide its age. They probably expect it before too long to become bulldozer bait, as have so many of its contemporaries on the blocks between our place and downtown. I doubt that a single passerby has even an inkling that the oak flooring in our old house by itself is likely worth more than the entire place appears to be.

Portis Ribble, my preacher/carpenter buddy, called unexpectedly just now as I was writing this paragraph. He still lives and ministers in San Angelo. I told him I was spinning a yarn that involved him. It may well be that he and I are the only humans alive who know just how valuable and beautiful is that original oak in the floor of that old house.

Chapter 2

The Dream

Just as soon as the bank note was paid off, the unpleasant era of tenants in the Key Place ended. By then, the series of struggling families who lived in the old house had desecrated it. In seven years they managed to do more damage than my grandparents and all their descendants had inflicted on the place in nearly half a century. My heart hurt when I saw the devastation. But, to tell the truth, the house was not in prime condition when I started renting it out. I knew even then that one day it would need extensive renovations, so I decided not to sweat the tenants' disregard for a place that meant so much to us.

Saying good-bye to the last tenant family was a jubilant time for me. On that day, I got serious about sprucing up the house and turning it into a place my family and I could enjoy. In the next few years, my three brothers and I spent many a happy day painting, paneling, glazing, plumbing, and generally upgrading that used-up old house into better shape than it had been in for years.

For the first time ever, carpet covered the floors, blown-on acoustic modernized the ceilings, and a wall heater warmed us in the winter. New cabinets with built-in appliances and a modern sink time-warped the kitchen from pre-Depression days to the present.

We brothers got excited as we completed each stage in the total redo on the long-neglected dwelling. In the back of all our minds burned a single driving purpose for all this expenditure of time and materials and labor. We could see that our parents were reaching an age when they likely would need to migrate out of Houston's traffic to a smaller, quieter, safer place. Where better for them than the house where our mother had spent her teen years? If nothing else, we thought, our parents at least could retreat to the refurbished, now-comfortable house for weeks at a time, enjoying its location not far from their own siblings and a host of other kinfolks.

As we tackled each new stage in the refurbishing project, we were energized by imagining the delight that would sparkle in our mother's eyes when she saw our handiwork in the house she loved so much. No place on earth was more precious to her than this one. Without a doubt, it was the key place in her life.

My Chevy pickup squatted low under the load of paneling I hauled south to begin covering walls marred by cracks that appeared when Grandmother was no longer there to pour precious water on the shrubs and flowers bordering the concrete foundation on all four sides of the house. For over two years, it took me every spare moment I could wangle to get that paneling installed, but those were blessed hours of glorious labor. Every joint was measured with precision, each sheet hung with loving care because I could see my mother's incredulity at how totally our work was transforming her old home.

So it was for every phase of our restoration of the house. Living so many miles away and all four of us loaded with family and ministry obligations, my brothers and I still found immense joy as the gradual makeover began to take shape. Even the work that would never be visible to a visitor's eyes—the plumbing, wiring, and structural upgrading—was the sort of thing we expected to thrill our mother, for she had lived in the house before it had indoor plumbing, or effective heating, or wall plugs throughout.

Only a person who had raised and lowered the double-hung wood-sash windows repeatedly for decades would appreciate the hours we spent carefully removing window facings throughout the house to replace frayed or broken ropes attached to the normally unseen window weights. What would our mother say when she spotted the modern kitchen cabinets we had installed to replace the homemade ones she and her mother had so totally used up?

Hot water had been a relatively late addition to the kitchen. A single 1940-vintage faucet had been added alongside the existing but not-quite-identical cold-water one, with the supply pipes for both faucets attached to the outside wall and poked through holes bored eight or nine inches above the ancient cast-iron sink, which now had blemishes marring its industrial-strength white porcelain.

All of that system—so prone to freezing on wintry days—was now replaced by a modern cabinet top with inside pipes and a fancy stainless steel, double-basin sink adorned with a modern Moen water mixer. We just knew that when our mother saw all of this, she would think she had died and gone to heaven.

The final stage was the carpet. Floors in the old house had been covered decade by decade with various kinds of linoleum and tile, layer upon layer in some cases, with a resulting irregularity of surface that made carpet the only right way to cover up the mess.

Years before, in the summer when I lived in Robert Lee and preached for my grandparents' little church, Nelan Bahlman had owned the only dry cleaning shop in town. That summer he and I became lifelong friends. Now, as we were completing the redo of the Key house, I knew that Nelan owned a fine hardware store in nearby Winters, Texas. So I asked him to come measure our floors, and then I bargained with him to send his floor man to carpet the house. Once this was done, all the damages inflicted by careless tenants and the even more extensive damage wrought by our own construction projects would be masked. The carpet would crown all the work my brothers and I had lavished on the place during the past half-dozen years.

We couldn't wait for Mom to see what we had done for her.

Such is the awesome power of a worthy dream.

Most of the grand achievements in this world likely would have remained unattempted except for the bold imaginings—the brilliantly lustrous dreams—that ignited the creative fires and fueled the faith of ordinary mortals, empowering them to do more and reach farther than anybody thought they could. Somewhere Martha Snell Nicholson wrote:

> *A dream has the lift of a lever,*
> *A dream has the power to drive.*

She was right.

I can't think of any other power or attraction sufficient to drag my brothers and me out of our pulpits and our studies, halfway across the endless expanse of Texas, to spend countless hot, dirty, arduous hours remodeling a broken-down old house we never planned to occupy. But the dream of so totally pleasing our mother transformed the unthinkable into the desirable for us.

How much poorer our world would be without the dreams that have inspired humanity to cross oceans, to reach for the stars, to dissect molecules, split atoms, and kill germs. Carl Sandburg counseled, "Woe unto him who believes in nothing. Always the impossible happens." Even if it doesn't, what does take shape as a result of our unfulfilled dreams often turns out to be more glorious than anything we dreamed of.

Early in my own ministry I discovered that I would always need a new mountain to climb. Just scaling the one at hand never satisfied me. One project was seldom completed before I found myself exploring two more—each peak higher than the last, each dream more exciting than the one before it.

Some would describe me as a workaholic. I prefer to be labeled a "dreamaholic." To that charge I gladly plead guilty. As my remaining years of full-time ministry dwindle, I find myself better understanding the famous quote attributed to South African pioneer Cecil John Rhodes near the end of his illustrious career: "So little time, so much to do." But I would add, "Hasn't it been fun so far?"

On a tombstone in a cemetery near Thurmont, Maryland, someone spotted an epitaph that says,

Here lies an Atheist
All dressed up
And no place to go.

That's sad, but atheists aren't the only people on earth who have "no place to go." Far too many believers in Jesus wander aimlessly through life—unexcited, limp-spirited, members of the bored—because evidently they have never heard the Savior's mandates to go, teach, feed, clothe, comfort, give, seek, love. They sense no calling worth their commitment, no ministry that stirs their active compassion, no vision that quickens their pulse and excites their souls.

In a series of cute letters purporting to be written by kids in a church school was one that said,

> *Dear God,*
> *I am doing the best I can. Really.*
> *Frank.*

Tragically, a lot of believers are not doing the best they can because they have never encountered the God whose presence and purposes would galvanize them to love him with *all* their heart and strength and mind and soul. Instead, what they have mistaken for God and his message and his people makes them yawn. It bores them.

Let me assure you that when the God of the Burning Bush calls your name, the one thing you will not be is bored. You may be scared out of your sandals, shaken to the roots of your soul, awestruck, and prostrate in the dust, but I promise, you won't be bored.

When the Galilean Captain of all Seas commissions you to fish for him, boredom will not be your first reaction. You may be looking hard for a nearby hole to hide in, anywhere to get away from the penetrating effulgence of his holiness. Like Peter, you may implore him, "Depart from me, Lord," but if you really meet God's holy Son, the days of lackadaisical, lethargic, uninvolved religion will be over. For he will demand all that you are—the best that you can be.

One of the finest descriptions of genuine Christianity was written by an Old Testament prophet and borrowed by the apostle Peter to describe the vitality of true faith in Jesus. When God brings us to his Son and fills us with his Spirit, then, both Joel and Peter assure us, "Your young men will see visions, your old men will dream dreams" (Acts 2:17 RSV). What a tragedy if we settle for a form of religion void of visions of how God is at work in our world and deprived of dreams about what he might do in our lives.

The Bible describes the patriarch Abraham as a man who was looking for a city "whose builder and maker was God" (to use the old King James wording of Hebrews 11:10). People who have truly been touched by the Lord are like that. They "seek the things that are above, where Christ is" (Col. 3:1 RSV). They store up their treasures in heaven instead of hoarding wealth here on earth. They dream what others might call "impossible dreams." Their hopes and plans have eternal dimensions, reaching far beyond what they presently can see or know.

"Is anything too hard for the LORD?" the angel asked Sarah when she snickered at God's plans for her (Gen. 18:14 NIV). When our goals and dreams are tied to a God like that, they tap into energies and uncover abilities we didn't know we had, just as the dream my brothers and I had of rebuilding our mother's old home stretched us to commit time and resources that would have seemed unthinkable except for that dream.

Alas, our dream was in vain. During the week when all the sawdust-making and painting were complete and the carpet was being laid—right when the project had reached the point where we hoped to proudly unveil all those months of loving labor to our mother—she became terribly ill. Doctors in Houston diagnosed the brain tumor that took her life less than a year later. Mom was never physically able to make the trip to see the house we had refurbished for her. She never got a glimpse of the place we had prepared for her to enjoy in her last years.

After that fateful week, our mother's only trip back home to Robert Lee was in a hearse. We transported her body to a plot in the Paint Creek Cemetery on land donated by her own homesteading grandfather almost two decades before she was born. After we had laid her to rest in the Coke County soil she had loved so fiercely, we returned to town, back to the house we had fixed up just for her. Somehow it seemed as empty as our hearts. When she died, our dream died too.

"The years forever fashion new dreams when old ones go," Robert Goddard once wrote. Then he exclaimed, "God pity the one-dream man!" An important part of life for all of us is redreaming old dreams to make them fit our changing world and also finding new ones to replace those that are no longer tenable.

As deflated as my brothers and I at first were by this unforeseen turn of events, still, all of our hard work and the hours we had spent improving our mother's homeplace were far from wasted. They just took us to an entirely different destination than the one we had envisioned—a destination that has turned out to be every bit as full of blessing as the one we were aiming for.

Life is often like this, isn't it?

A few years ago I keynoted the annual seminar of our local chapter of the Inspirational Writers Association. The theme of one of my presentations was the seldom confessed truth that those of us who write professionally often have little or no idea where we are headed when we start putting words on paper.

My speech was largely an episode of "True Confessions of an Addled Author" (although I titled it more properly "Through a Glass Dimly"), for, more often than not, this is my writing strategy.

More times than I can tell you I have hunkered down at the keyboard and started off a weekly newspaper column with a good attention grabber, thinking I had at least a general idea where I was headed with my topic, only to have it take a detour two or three short paragraphs later. In some cases I ended up making a point that had been entirely off my scope when I started writing. This does not mean my column was ruined. Often I stumbled into a fortuitous message I never would have conveyed otherwise. Whether we're writing columns or remodeling ancestral houses, we don't always arrive where we thought we would.

If my column writing appears unfocused, I told my inspirational writing students that day, my approach to writing books must appear even more haphazard. Most of my books have begun with random chapters which at the time had no visible connection one to the other.

My first book, *The God Who Puts Us Back Together,* serves as a good example. It did not start out as a book. Over several years of ministry I had written (and then preached) eight or nine seemingly unconnected true stories about people whose lives had crossed mine. Writing those tales was fun for me, and the people I preach to seemed to enjoy the occasional change of pace from "straight" sermons.

One day I sat shuffling through that stack of stories, wondering if they had any common thread that could tie them together. And suddenly I saw it. Each tale was about some person with a broken life or a shattered dream. Only then, years after it began, did I know that I was well along the road toward writing a book about human brokenness.

Not everybody writes this way, I quickly admitted to my seminar students. Some authors are more focused. Better organized. They see farther down the road than I can, even when the road bends. But starting off without knowing where I am going just happens to be my usual method of writing.

I shared this confession with that band of wannabe writers, hoping to encourage them to get busy writing without waiting to analyze and outline every detail they intend to present. For some of us, I told them, writing is not like plotting a distant path with a telescope. It is more like driving on a dark road in a blinding blizzard. All we need to see is the edge of the road and the next few feet in front of us. Part of the delight of writing like this lies in finally discovering what unexpected place we have come to.

Perhaps (in fact, almost certainly) I am an odd duck as a writer, but I do suspect that the blind-writing approach I have just described is far more common than beginning writers might suppose.

Several years ago now, when Frank Peretti was hard at work on his novel *The Visitation*, his publisher was scrambling to get it to market by the inexorable spring deadline. They enlisted several of us to help them come up with just the right title for the book he had not finished yet. All we had in hand were the early chapters in typewritten, manuscript form, and we were strictly warned not to show those pages to any living soul because Peretti had not yet decided just how his plot would unfold.

Yes! I exclaimed in my soul. Here is a big-name, high-dollar author who writes just like I do. He starts down the path without knowing exactly where it may take him.

For many of us who write, the only way to learn our destination is to start writing and see where we wind up. Only God knows where we're headed.

You have heard, haven't you, how The Living Bible came to be? Dr. Kenneth Taylor didn't set out to translate the Bible or to write a best-selling paraphrase of Scripture. When he read Bible stories to his kids, they couldn't fathom the quaint syntax of the King James Version. So Taylor, with no vision beyond that brief daily task, set about paraphrasing short segments of Scripture for each evening's family study, replacing jawbreaker words and archaic terms with shorter, more familiar vocabulary his kids could understand.

Night by night, segment by segment, this godly man paraphrased snippets of Scripture, until at last he had simplified a good portion of the Bible. Friends who saw his work began to urge him to share it with a broader audience. Only then did he begin to work at a faster pace with a grander goal of a Bible that could be understood by an entire generation. Without intending to at first, this man of God had produced the most widely read Bible of his time.

So it was with our project to restore our mother's homeplace. The dream of pleasing our mother and providing for her later years was a noble aim that kept us pumped up and focused on the job at hand. But her untimely death forced us to radically refocus our reasons for investing time and dollars and labor on a small, aging residence hundreds of miles from our own front doors.

How marvelous it is to have a God who knows where we need to go before we do.

M Louise Haskins wrote a memorable vignette about trusting in God when we are uncertain about where we are going. In an almost poetic way she advised that we can walk with confidence down the road of life, for although we cannot see over the hill or around the bend, we hold the hand of One who can.

How wisely and benevolently the Master Planner guided my brothers and me. All that time we thought we were fashioning the ultimate gift for our mother, when we were in fact preparing the perfect place for us to retreat from our crushing ministry demands—a place where we could slow down, regroup, and read and write and pray and play.

Each of my first four books reached critical mass during days of quietness and reflection I spent alone in and around this house we meant for our mother. Only God knows how many of my newspaper columns in the past decades germinated right here in this nondescript dwelling.

For us brothers the Key Place has become a place to rekindle our creative fires, a place to produce massive blocks of work in a fraction of the time it would take amid normal workday interruptions.

As I write this paragraph, my oldest brother B. is the "pastor in residence" at the Key Place, enjoying a blessed two-week stint. And the rest of us are jealous. We seldom manage to get away to Robert Lee for more than three or four days per visit.

In two weeks my brother B. will churn out more course outlines, promotional material, monthly newsletter copy, and brotherhood correspondence than he could produce in two months in his office in the big, busy city where he normally labors. Two weeks from now he will resume an impossible workload at home, refreshed, rejuvenated, rested in a way he seldom can be while wearing the hats he chooses to wear.

Meanwhile, we other brothers—Curtis and Jim and I—read our elder brother's emails from the Key Place with a wistful yearning to be there beside him, reading the latest Philip Yancey or Max Lucado book in the shade of the Arizona cypress, or just supervising the young finches and cardinals as they learn mature dining etiquette at the always busy bird feeder outside the kitchen window. Each of us would surely agree that few things have blessed our souls more than this modest little house we thought we were rebuilding for our mother. Without doubt it has become the key place in each of our lives.

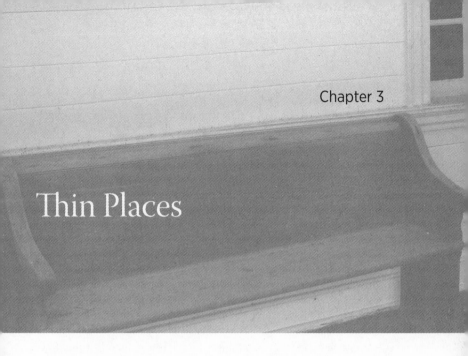

Chapter 3

Thin Places

In their ancient myths the Celtic people talked about "thin places" in the universe, places where the physical and spiritual realms come closer than usual to each other. Wise and good people welcome such places. They even seek them. For these are the places where those of us in this world are most likely to discern the truths of the world beyond us. Harvard's chaplain Dr. Peter Gomes calls these threshold places—also using the terms *border* or *frontier* places—where the seen and unseen worlds momentarily touch one another.

We might stand in such a place when people with exceptional gifts from God touch our lives with their music or their poetry, or with simple kindnesses, so that we tremble inside. Times of intense suffering may take us to the edge of our world—to a thin place—as might moments of mystery and awe in worship. When Jacob slept on the stone that night in Bethel, he saw heaven opened and the Lord God Almighty perched atop a stairway where angels were coming and going while Jacob watched. "Surely this is where God lives," he exclaimed.

Identifying such places seems to be more common in the holidays. When Thanksgiving softens our hearts and Christmas brings merriment to our souls, God seems able to draw more intimately near to us. Every Thanksgiving when our eyes turn gratefully toward heaven, the gap between us and God somehow narrows. Every time the music and messages of Christmas remind us that God once stepped over the border of heaven and walked as a man upon earth, the excitement of this truth entices us nearer to the boundary between the two realms. This may explain the warmth and joy and deep satisfaction that flood our souls year after year during the final great holidays on our calendars.

Holidays that close the gap between us and God might more accurately be called thin *times* instead of thin *places*. But most of us can identify actual physical places where we feel that we can "reach out and touch the face of God," as the poet John Magee put it.

When the patriarch Abraham reached the land God had promised to him, he constructed a series of altars—first at Shechem, then at Bethel, and later at Hebron—places where he communed with the God who had drawn him to that land. In later life, he and his offspring would return to those same key places to renew their link with their God.

Years later, Moses discovered that Mount Sinai was another such place where God was present for him in a special way. Barefooted before the burning bush, Moses first heard the voice of his fathers' God. Many months later, with all of Israel encamped at its base, Moses scaled the holy mountain while thunder rolled and trumpets blared and the rocks shook beneath his feet. Hidden there in the smoke and clouds that shrouded that holy place, the old prophet watched as the finger of the Almighty etched His covenant on stone. For Moses this was a thin place—a place where God drew near.

In the centuries that followed, Jerusalem with Solomon's famous temple perched on Mount Zion was such a place for many generations. The psalmists rather quaintly referred to it as "God's holy hill." And the Gospels implied that the mountain where Peter, James, and John saw Christ transfigured was another such spot.

The fact that these three holy mountains appear in Scripture should not lead us to conclude that locations like these are limited to distant places in ancient eras. Most men and women of faith in every age can point to special places where God has made his presence known to them.

For at least the last half of my life, the Key Place has been a thin place for me. Once or twice a year we four brothers gang up and come here, mostly just to enjoy some relaxed hours together, but also more often than not to tackle some upkeep project—painting trim, patching plumbing, pruning trees, building fence, grubbing prickly pear. We're never short of jobs that need doing. But the times I cherish most are those when I slip down to this quiet old house alone. Sequestered here with no telephone to answer, no television to watch, no radio to distract me, and no other human present to invade my thoughts, I connect with the Lord and feel his Spirit as I seldom do anywhere else.

My dear friend and favorite nun, Sister Olivia Prendergast, in her last months told me of a time when she had elected to withdraw into seclusion and silence at a spiritual retreat center in the open ranch country of deep South Texas.

Before the catchphrase 24/7 had been coined to describe the job assignment of us workaholics, dear Olivia had put in those hours for the larger part of a decade. At the prime of her health and full of spiritual fire, she had burst upon us in Amarillo with a passionate vision for compassionate medical and spiritual care for people who are dying. In a flurry of seminars, classes, newspaper articles, and one-on-one briefings, Olivia taught us the meaning of "hospice." With the tenacity of Lee Iacocca and the single-minded compassion of Mother Teresa, Olivia hounded the leaders of our hospitals and our city until, together, we established one of the hallmark hospice programs in the world.

In the last months of her leadership at our hospice, however, Olivia's fervor waned. Her spiritual fires flickered. Changes in administrative personnel and hospital policies put her under fire—right at a time when the imminent death of her father in Ireland required her presence and much of her energy. As she confided her frustrations to me, I thought I detected in her the telltale signs of burnout. Her surprise resignation from both the organization she had founded and the leadership position she had loved confirmed my fears.

Almost as quickly as she had come into my life, Olivia vanished from my Protestant eyes into the labyrinth known best to Catholic nuns who need repair. Years later, as I worked with her to edit the delightful book that bears her name, Olivia told me that she coped with her burnout by spending several weeks at that South Texas retreat under a vow of silence. Hearing few words and speaking none, she focused on God and allowed the silence slowly to mend her used-up, wounded soul.

In the fruitful years of service that followed, whenever Olivia thought of those silent days, she would smile and speak wistfully of her desire to return to that blessed retreat center, which for her had been a thin place—a place where God broke through.

Olivia's experience in that silent place was not unlike my own some years before—right here at the Key Place. As she told me her tale, I remembered my own close scrape with burnout—a hectic period some twenty-plus years ago—when my own inner resources were running so low that I was perilously close to spiritual implosion. For several years I had been working too hard, running too fast, spreading my creative energies way too thin, and it finally caught up with me.

Not only was I insanely over-obligated (mostly my own doing), but I was weary of putting up with some of the foolishness embedded in our ways of doing church. In his second letter to the Corinthian church, the apostle Paul stopped at one point and said to them, "I wish that you would bear with me in a little foolishness" (11:1 NASB). The foolishness Paul referred to here was his tongue-in-cheek boasting when he listed his credentials as an apostle, most of them real scars and proofs of suffering.

I don't want to boast about anything, satirically or otherwise. But I would like to borrow the apostle's words to observe right here that anybody who spends much time around a church has to "bear with a little foolishness." We church folks do some silly things in the name of Christ. I don't say this out of bitterness or to criticize the church. It's just a fact we need to recognize out loud every so often as we chuckle at our own addled antics and peculiar pieties we call "church work."

Did I just receive a message from heaven? Or could it have been a temptation from Satan? I'll let you decide. I had just written the last few sentences about the foolishness preachers and church people have to put up with when a delivery van pulled up outside my church office and the driver knocked on our door. He came to deliver a new supply of freshly printed bulletin covers. I was glad to see him because I had let us almost run out before remembering to reorder.

The helpful young man wheeled in the heavy boxes and cheerfully hoisted them into place so this gray-haired old man wouldn't have to do it. I had signed his invoice and sent him hurriedly on his way when I looked down at my copy of the invoice. The typist at the print shop had intended to type "Church Bulletins" in the product column, but she had hit the wrong keys and then used white-out to cover her mistakes on both copies of the invoice. I'm sure that the top copy—the copy they kept for their records—reads correctly, but on the bottom copy of the carbonless set, the one they left with us, the carbon had failed to imprint the corrections on that layer of white-out. So my copy of the invoice says as plain as day that we just purchased ten thousand copies of "Church Bull." Precisely what I was writing about before that timely delivery.

Before that serendipitous interruption, I was about to confess to you that at that particular time years ago in my ministry I was running on low, almost out of spiritual fuel, and consequently I was far more nettled than I normally would have been by some of the sanctified silliness that was making my job in ministry a whole lot harder than it should have been.

Discouraged, angry, threadbare in my soul, I found myself barely able to plod through the minimal duties required of me. I was used up and didn't realize it until almost too late. My ministry—at least my ministry where I now have served more than four and a half decades—might well have ended long before my most fruitful years had I not been able to retreat to the Key Place to get away from it all and to replenish my lagging spirit.

I recall one warm autumn night during those days. All that afternoon I had worked hard in the hot Robert Lee sun, weed-eating, cutting brush, cleaning fence rows—deliciously satisfying physical labor compared to the long, strenuous hours of head-and-heart involvement that made up my usual workday at home. I was tired, but it was a good tiredness.

After a leisurely hamburger at the Cracker Barrel, I wandered back up to the house about dusk. At sundown the air outside was beginning to cool down, but we had not air conditioned the old house and the Lord was not providing enough breeze that evening to let me work comfortably inside. So I hauled a folding metal chair down into the patch near the bois d'arc tree, and I sat there—doing absolutely nothing—as I watched the last rays of the sun vanishing behind a deck of clouds low on the western horizon and one by one the stars peeking out of the darkening sky.

For the longest time I lingered there motionless, soaking up the quietness of the evening, dreaming unrealistically of how marvelous it would be to do this every day, every evening. My meager income from two or three old rental houses would more than cover the taxes and utilities on the Key Place, I calculated. Food was cheap here. Surely, I told myself, I could scrounge up enough book editing and book jacket copywriting to survive. I could hole up here away from all the demands that were stealing my happiness and sapping my soul.

My fantasies that evening were the typically irrational ones of a person going through the meltdown of burnout. I had reached the stage where just about any option looked better than the daily duties I normally loved so much. I was ready to chuck it all and vanish to some place where nobody knew my phone number or address. Right at that moment I couldn't think of a better place than right where I sat.

Just how long I roosted there in that chair in the patch I don't know. The almost full moon was now rising. Big. Bright. White. It was lighting up the fresh-mown weeds across the patch, but I was shielded from its direct light, perched in the dark blob of shadows cast by the bois d'arc tree and the ancient mesquite tree that sprawls out on the north end of the patch.

Suddenly down to the right my eye caught a whisk of light close by. I froze, fortunately. Out of the shadows between my chair and the fence along the creek bed sauntered the biggest skunk I had ever laid eyes on. With his white-striped tail held arrogantly high and waggling in the moonlight, he pranced within three feet of me. One move on my part and he surely would have doused me with his unique perfume. I hardly dared to breathe until he sidled across the patch and disappeared under the fence back into the dry creek bed from whence he had come.

I can't testify with any certainty that the good Lord sent that critter to visit me, but I can guarantee you that his unexpected appearance instantly cut short any ruminations I might have been having about job pressures back at home.

The Lord did speak to me during my retreats to the Key Place that fall. No, I am not telling you that I heard audible voices or saw visions or anything like that. I am neither an apostle nor the son of an apostle, to parody Amos's famous line. But the Lord spoke to me plainly during those blessedly quiet days and addressed the distress of my harried heart.

The prophet Isaiah was right when he told his people, "In quietness and trust is your strength" (30:15). The only way God can get through to us sometimes is for us to hush up and listen. "Be still, and know that I am God," he bids us (Ps. 46:10 KJV). Some of us are never "still" on the inside. In our hearts and minds, anxieties churn, hostilities boil, demands echo, fears ferment—and there are times when we don't know how to turn off this commotion in our souls.

I'm convinced that the only solution for this internal noise may be purposeful times of silence—times when we retreat both from the torrent of information and demands bombarding us from every quarter and from the requirement that we respond continually to spouses, bosses, relatives, neighbors, and friends. The psalmist prescribed good medicine for us when he advised, "Search your hearts and be silent" (4:4). The fellow who wrote Ecclesiastes was badly mixed up about most of life, but he told the truth when he wrote that there is "a time to be silent" (3:7).

This is when God spoke to my heart and offered solutions to my mounting frustrations and mental fatigue—during the times when I withdrew to this isolated plot of family land, this key place in my world, where I could hibernate for three or four days at a time, seldom speaking a dozen words a day or hearing as many. During those silent days God spoke and the Spirit moved.

In one of our cherished Christmas carols we sing,

> *How silently, how silently*
> *The wondrous gift is given.*
> *So God imparts to human hearts*
> *The blessings of His heaven.*

Holy silence is one of the dominant marks of thin places. I never get tired of visiting the grand cathedrals of Europe and Great Britain. As you know, far too many of those majestic churches sit empty most of the time. Finding run-over Sunday morning crowds at St. Paul's and at Westminster Abbey in London thrilled me, but my heart aches when I see magnificent places of worship such as Notre Dame and Chartres filled with crowds of gawking tourists instead of worshippers.

All across the Continent we have observed this phenomenon, but a closer look in almost every cathedral revealed to me a handful of devout believers, often on their knees, deep in prayer in the huge quietness of what to them is still a holy place. Oblivious to us tourists who invade their place of prayer, they appear to be lost in a personal reverie that is enhanced by the muted silence inside those vast stone walls. They are in touch with their Creator in what for them is a thin place.

Anybody who has set foot in Robert Lee, Texas, will likely find it hilariously outlandish that I have implied even the slightest link between this unpretentious West Texas town and the famous cathedral cities of Europe. The largest church building in Robert Lee would get lost in the foyer of St. Peter's, and the whole town—believers and pagans combined—would fit into the sanctuary with all sorts of room to spare.

My only point of comparison is that Europe's finest cathedrals and the Key Place in Robert Lee draw the same clientele—people hungry for quiet time with the Lord. I hope those solitary worshippers we saw on the pews at Chartres or Canterbury were finding as much solace there as I have found here in Robert Lee in the shadow of this old house.

Thin places come in all shapes and sizes for people who are equally diverse. The apostle Paul told the truth about God when he preached, "He is not far from each one of us" (Acts 17:27b RSV).

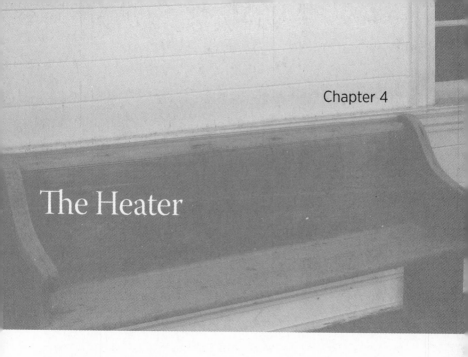

Chapter 4

The Heater

Because I love the Key Place so dearly and because I express so much delight in the precious days I get to spend here, I find that I have misled some of my readers and associates.

My dear friend and Bible student Elizabeth Nussbaum read and heard so much from me about this favorite hideaway that she decided to use her highly acclaimed artistic talents to capture the Key Place in oil on canvas. Just provide her a photo or two, she offered, and she would get busy painting.

I'm not sure what Elizabeth expected. Possibly that this special place must be an elegant chateau tucked away on a choice tract of land. Nothing could be much further from the truth. I remember the surprised look on her face when she first saw pictures of this plain-Jane, minuscule old house perched atop three nondescript acres bordered by ancient fences and adorned by at least three decades of landscaping by the accidents of a climate that most of the time tends to be too hot, too cold, or too dry for all but the hardiest of God's herbage.

Proving her prowess as an artist, Elizabeth's painting of my mother's homeplace endowed it with the elegance and grace we Key descendants see in it, while the neighbors who drive by it surely must see only an aging hovel. I thought of Elizabeth's rendition of the Key Place when I drove up to the front door last night just after the sun had gone down. This is the first time I have been here since this dear lady unveiled her work of love. (Her fine painting now fills the main wall of my church study.)

I came here this time expecting spring to be in full bloom. In fact, I checked the long-term weather forecast to see if this week might turn out to be uncomfortably warm. Instead I was greeted by a final blast of arctic air that sneaked in on me. The thermometer in my PT Cruiser read 38 when I pulled up beside the front gate. Before this morning's dawn, the lady at the convenience store just told me, the mercury had dipped down to 26.

Usually I come to Robert Lee from the Texas Panhandle, so I know what kind of weather will be sliding in from the north while I'm here. But this time I drove in from Houston—from the opposite direction—and I got blindsided by this last gasp of winter. When I started unloading my gear and going through the usual wintertime routine to open up the place, I realized quickly that I was not dressed for it. By the time I got the water turned on and the water heater filled so that I could switch on the electricity and get enough light to see how to fire up the heater, I was cold to the bone and shivering all over. Did that heater ever feel good!

With a pot of coffee brewing on the stove and the wall heater cranked up full bore, a blessed warmth soon began to conquer the chill. Before long I forgot how cold I had been. Several times during the rest of the evening, though, I found myself recalling my first years in this old house and remembering how bone-chilling cold it could be in the dead of winter.

My Key grandparents made no effort to heat any portion of the house except the kitchen. The old wood-sash windows were so loose—and, as in most houses of this vintage, there were so many of them—that the arctic winds came right on inside. With no insulation overhead to keep the warmth from leaking out through the attic, it would have been impossible to warm up all of the rooms in the old house anyway. So on winter nights we slept under piles of heavy quilts and blankets, afraid to poke out even our noses for fear of frostbite.

In its earliest days (long before I was born) my grandparents heated the place with a wood-burning stove. The brick chimney that shielded its smokestack still rests out of sight in the attic on rafters above the southeast corner of the kitchen. By the time I came along, though, the Key Place was uptown and modern. Granddaddy had installed a fancy new kerosene stove (probably the most dangerous form of home heating ever known to man). I remember that the stove was UPS brown, long before anybody had heard of UPS.

On those icy winter mornings Granddaddy would rise long before the rest of us. From the grandchildren's pallet in the frigid living room I could hear him clumping in and out the back door as he ventured out into the vicious cold to refill the stove's kerosene reservoir from the storage barrel in the chicken patch.

During the winter months this was an every-morning ritual. It was the only way to enjoy any heat inside the house. And it was a job only my grandfather could do. When the five-gallon kerosene tank was full, it was too heavy for any of us kids or for the ladies to handle. And the danger of mishandling that much kerosene near a stove ruled out most of the city-slicker male relatives who had enough brawn to handle the job.

In all those years of getting frozen stiff morning after winter morning at the kerosene barrel, not once did I hear my grandfather complain. If he said anything, it was to tell us how grateful he was to have a stove that worked so much better than the woodburner that preceded it.

Have you noticed that a big part of our being properly thankful today depends on our ability to remember yesterday?

Despite the deceitful ploys of politicians trying to make us unhappy with our present lot, I can affirm without hesitation that year after year—decade after decade—I have been better off than I was in the previous period. In my young adult years, for example, I had no choice but to drive someone else's cast-off clunker. For a long time, in a multi-car world, ours was a single-car family. But with each automobile trade, our wheels have improved.

It would be easy for me to cast an envious eye on some friend's expensive SUV and stalk away complaining that my vehicles are nowhere near that class. Could that be why number ten on God's top list of commandments is "You shall not covet"? Whether we covet our neighbor's donkey (a la the original Exodus prohibitions) or his Cadillac Escalade, the result is still the same. It robs us of delight in our own present possessions.

Right now as I write these words I'm the proud owner of a burgundy PT Cruiser, which has to be the sportiest vehicle and the most fun to drive of all the cars I've ever owned. What a shame if my pleasure in my Cruiser were to be sullied because I started coveting my doctor-neighbor's Lamborghini.

Present thankfulness is always enhanced when we recall past hardships.

Today's plenty provokes gratitude when compared to yesterday's exigencies.

My wise grandfather modeled this. Instead of fussing about all the inconveniences and potential dangers of his kerosene heater, all he had to do was to recall the hours he had spent splitting and hauling wood for his far less efficient wood-burning stove.

Clear memories provoke genuine thanksgiving.

Sometimes I suspect that I'm a slow learner. It took me longer than it should have to realize that my own happiness depends almost totally not on what I possess at the moment, but on how thankful I am for those present possessions. Maybe this is why Ambrose of Milan centuries ago warned his flock, "No duty is more urgent than that of returning thanks." Years later, but still a long time before you and I came along, William Temple identified thankfulness as one of the keys to happiness. "It is probable," he wrote, "that in most of us the spiritual life is impoverished and stunted because we give so little place to gratitude. It is more important to thank God for blessings received than to pray for them beforehand. For that forward-looking prayer, though right as an expression of dependence upon God, is still self-centered in part, at least, of its interest; there is something we hope to gain by our prayer. But the backward-looking act of thanksgiving is quite free from this. In itself it is quite selfless. Thus it is akin to love. All our love to God is in response to his love for us; it never starts on our side. 'We love, because he first loved us' (1 John 4:19)."

As a youngster I did not realize what a priceless gift God had given my Grandfather Key when he endowed him with a genuinely grateful heart. He lived most of his days without most of the modern comforts we tend to consider essential today. Instead of bemoaning the discomfort and hard work inherent to his modest lifestyle, I often heard my grandfather expressing his genuine pleasure in getting to use and enjoy the latest upgrade in some tool or appliance or piece of equipment essential to his work.

I doubt my granddad ever heard of G. K. Chesterton, but he certainly subscribed to that famous Englishman's philosophy of thanksgiving.

> *You say grace before meals.*
> *All right.*
> *But I say grace before the play and the opera,*
> *And grace before the concert and pantomime,*
> *And grace before I open a book,*
> *And grace before sketching, painting,*
> *Swimming, fencing, boxing, walking, playing, dancing;*
> *And grace before I dip the pen in the ink.*

All of us would be happier and surely we would be easier to be around if we "said grace" before every experience heaven allows us to enjoy and over every possession we have been allowed to hold.

The Scriptures enjoin such a grateful spirit. "In everything give thanks; for this is God's will for you in Christ Jesus" (1 Thess. 5:18 NASB). One major stimulus to such thanksgiving lies in recognizing how much today surpasses yesterday.

Today *is* better than yesterday. Far better. In countless ways the aging and exceedingly modest house on the Key Place stands as irrefutable evidence that each generation of God-fearing people will leave the world a better place for those who follow after them.

Sometime not long after World War II, butane became the fuel of choice on Coke County ranches and rural homes. I'm sure it immediately became my grandfather's choice. With gas piped in from the big butane tank that stood in the chicken patch, all he had to do on those frightfully frigid winter mornings was to strike a match and turn a valve to light an efficient stove without ever setting foot outside the house.

My clearest childhood memories revolve around that labor-intensive, bone-chilling kerosene model. I can still see us—my siblings and my cousins and whoever else among the kinfolks might have shown up for the occasion—all of us crammed cheek to cheek into that small kitchen since it was the only warm room in the house. The entire clan would huddle as close as possible to that kerosene stove, toasting one side of our bodies while, on the coldest days, the other side shivered.

That butane stove was an immense improvement, and yet it was only one more step along the road in the saga of the Key Place heaters.

Last night I sat at the kitchen table answering a slew of emails and finishing a newspaper column I had started writing before I left to go to Houston. While I labored over the keyboard of my laptop computer, the warmth from our modern double-sided natural gas wall heater quickly and easily heated the entire house.

How amazed and grateful Granddaddy Key would be, I thought, if he could see just this one improvement to the house he maintained and modernized by stages during the almost fifty years he owned it. Of all the upgrading and improving we grandkids have done since his death, I suspect he would tag the wall heater as the one change that would have blessed him the most.

As I wrote that last line, though, it dawned on me that I might be totally wrong. Maybe my assessment is flawed by my own generation's obsession with comfort.

My wife's recent Honda Odyssey just happened to come equipped with bum warmers, and during the cold winters we sometimes endure in Amarillo, this may have been the one gizmo on her fancy new van that pleased her the most. In my wildest reckoning I cannot imagine my grandfather being favorably impressed with such a frivolous feature on a vehicle. For this present generation of buyers I understand that it's a must-have item. And this may demonstrate the vast difference between his generation and ours.

Folks back then knew how to tolerate discomfort far better than we do. Having never known the at-your-fingertips comfort controls in modern automobiles, offices, homes, and churches, people in the pre-1950 world simply did not expect and demand comfort the way we do.

We twenty-first-century softies whose Western, civilized world has always been pain free, climate-controlled, air-bagged, sanitized, homogenized, Muzaked, flame-retarded, Sanforized, child-proof, and much too well fed seldom reflect on the fact that of all earth's generations, we are the exception. Historically, our generation is an anomaly—the best fed, best doctored, most comfortable, least endangered generation ever. And even now on a planet where well over half the present population exists in primitive squalor without the modern medical, transportation, and communication luxuries we take for granted, we are the odd ones. We alone are the comfortable, the coddled, and most of us who have it so good seem to assume that our user-friendly world is the norm. How could our perceptions possibly be more wrong?

Don't misunderstand what I'm trying to say here. I'm glad my doctor has an arsenal of medications and technologies at his disposal. Without them I would have died long ago. I like my air-conditioned, shock-absorbed, noise-abated auto far better than the rattletraps of my childhood.

I have no desire to live in a cave or a grass hut. Even with three-buck-a-gallon gasoline, I'm not ready to trade in my wheels for a donkey. My cell phone only works part of the time, but it surely does beat smoke signals or pony express. Given my diet preferences, I love the food supply system of our land that allows me to continue gorging myself even in times of drought or crop failure.

Nothing I am saying here implies any desire on my part to surrender the prosperity and ease of the society we live in. And I am not suggesting—not even hinting—that we who have been so blessed should debase ourselves in some kind of self-loathing because our land enjoys advantages other less-enlightened cultures have failed to develop for their people.

I am simply admitting that we middle-class, modern Americans do not view life from the perspective of most of humanity, either past or present. Because of the radical disconnect between our world and theirs, I seriously wonder if it is possible for us to sympathize with either our ancestors or our present global neighbors for whom daily reality entails high levels of danger and deprivation and discomfort.

That remarkable Jewish atheist-turned-Christian, Richard Wurmbrand, in his book *Christ on the Jewish Road* offers a curious comment on our generation's love affair with wealth and ease: "When God chose a language in which to express His revelations in the Bible, He chose the Hebrew language, possibly the only language in which the verb 'to have' does not exist" (206). It would be hard to describe our present life in such a language, wouldn't it?

My brother Curtis and I are sitting at the kitchen table in the Key house late one evening as I write these words. On his Dell laptop the two of us just now viewed a series of photos taken recently in Ugandan villages by his sons, Josh and Stephan, as they were enrolling AIDS orphans in a Christian care program. Although they live in mud hovels with grass roofs, the children and adult villagers in picture after picture are smiling and appear to be happy.

On the best village buildings in the photos I could see serious cracks in mud walls of buildings roofed with aging, rusting, weather-twisted, often-reused metal. Not one of the structures in the photos would be allowed to stand for long in an American community, but the Ugandan villagers in the pictures probably feel blessed to have homes or churches that good. In our luxurious corner of Earth we can't begin to get inside the hearts and heads of people like these, who survive on less than three hundred dollars a year.

Likewise, it is equally hard for most of us to imagine what it must have been like to live in the childhood world of my Grandfather Key, a world without electricity, radio, paved roads, gas-powered vehicles, refrigeration, indoor plumbing—and the list goes on endlessly. Such a world sounds like a nightmare to my grandchildren, but from my grandfather, from his siblings, or from his parents I never heard a word of complaint. They were quick to say that they had enjoyed a good life.

Could it be that the very conveniences and comforts you and I value so highly have robbed us of the priceless art of being content with far less?

When that good church in Philippi sent the apostle Paul a much-needed gift to sustain him during his imprisonment, he wrote his famous Philippian letter to thank them. Their gift blessed him, and he appreciated it, he said, but he was quick to assure them that he would have made it just fine without it. "I have learned to get along with a little bit or a lot," he wrote. "I have learned to be content in all circumstances, whether good or bad."

How many of us in our pampered age could truthfully make such a claim?

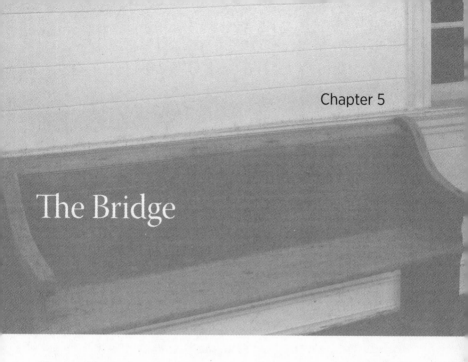

Chapter 5

The Bridge

The road used to end right in front of this old house. One night when the usually dry creek turned as nasty as a Brahma bull with mesquite thorns in his tail, the wild waters swept away the substantial concrete bridge which had spanned the draw that marks the western boundary of the Key Place. Not once but twice in the 1930s and '40s floodwaters undermined the low-budget concrete bridges that extended Ninth Street from the heart of Robert Lee to the west perimeter of the town.

By the time I was old enough to run and play in that creek-bed paradise, the road builders had cried calf rope. They had surrendered to Mother Nature. By then the former bridges were only a memory in the minds of older folks. Now the road ended right there in front of my grandparents' home. We had a cul-de-sac before any of us West Texans knew that term.

During the summers when I was seven and eight, my mother's parents invited me to spend a week with them in this house, which at that time was still in the prime of its life. My uncle—their youngest child—was back home from the Army Air Corps by then.

America and her allies had won World War II, so they no longer needed Uncle David to wash the blood out of the gun turrets and patch the flak holes in the battle-battered B-25s that hobbled home from England to North Carolina to be hastily refurbished and returned to the bombardment of Germany. He and my grandfather were busy hauling sheep, raising goats, and opening the first agricultural feed store in the county in a brand-new Main Street building with Purina's famous red-and-white checkerboard squares emblazoned on its facade and down both sides.

One of my clearest memories from those halcyon days is my grandfather's cattle truck circled into its accustomed parking place with its tall, long trailer snaked along the back edge of that gravel cul-de-sac and the nose of the cab stopped even with the galvanized-pipe gate that sixty years later still guards the sidewalk entrance to the house.

A winding footpath led due west from the cul-de-sac—where the road used to run—quickly losing itself in a thicket of prickly pears, mesquite bushes, and drought-stunted weeds, until that sandy path plunged precipitously toward the creek bottom twenty feet or so below. At its steepest point going down the bank nearest the house, the path zigzagged drunkenly to dodge an irregular outcropping of concrete—all that was left of the abutment for the last bridge, whose dismembered fragments now littered the creek in unrecognizable chunks scattered half a mile downstream by the frenzied floodwaters several years before I was born.

Westward beyond the creek, almost as far as my six-year-old frame would let me see, lay a section of land with only an old house or two on its far west edge, and in between stood an unbroken sea of brush—mainly mesquite trees and prickly pears—a perfect, unplanned preserve for cottontails and skunks and possums and coons. Even an occasional bobcat or coyote peeked out of that untouched territory.

But for lots of hours in those gloriously unstructured summers, that plot of unsettled land became the magical domain of five little boys—my older brother B. and my three Robert Lee cousins and me—playing everything from cowboys and Indians to big-game hunters with Boy Scout hatchets and Daisy BB guns. No theme park dreamed up by Disney and his ilk in the decades to follow could come close to what we enjoyed on the banks of that creek. Fancy places like Disneyland reflect some professional's imagination. There, in and around that private creek bed, the terrain morphed—sometimes several times a day—to fit whatever make-believe activity we declared to be operative for that moment, and the only limits on the scene changes were our own robust imaginations.

One chilly autumn night over half a century later my brothers and I sat roasting marshmallows over a small mesquite bonfire in the fire pit we built in what used to be the chicken patch behind the house. That night B. and I began reminiscing aloud about the glorious summer days we had spent as boys on that rugged real estate I just described to you.

Little brothers Curtis and Jim, who came along about the time I was finishing high school and starting college, listened with amazement. They shared none of our memories. By the time they were born, the bridge-eating creek had been tamed by a series of diversion dams upstream. Even during the heaviest rains, today it runs only a temporary trickle. Long before Jim and Curtis were old enough to scout out the territory west of the Key Place, the twisted, steep path into and out of the creek bed had been buried under the westward extension of the city street, its roadbed now firmly and permanently set in place over huge metal culvert pipes.

The younger guys had never known the quiet, private cul-de-sac of my youth. Their only memory was a rather busy public street stretching from Main Street to the city limits.

With that road had come the inevitable encroachment of civilization, as one by one houses were erected along each side of it. When I became the owner of the Key Place, for the first ten years or so I purposely kept our side of the creek bed (between us and those new houses) as wild and woolly as possible. The impenetrable stand of bamboo cane and mesquite brush shielded us from the growing residential area west of our property.

That band of wilderness in the modern creek bed blesses lots of wee critters by providing them safe habitat, and the purposely neglected brush barrier blesses us humans, too, allowing us on our side to sit there right in town while enjoying the feel that we still live out in the boonies.

Before my younger brothers were old enough to start to school, Robert Lee had begun its evolution from a rustic cow town to a citified municipality. The delicious darkness through which the stars blazed so brightly in the skies of my own childhood now began to be polluted with the glare of mercury vapor streetlights sprouting on street corners like April dandelions, welcomed by the local residents, I'm sure, but silently mourned by those of us who come to the small town to escape the blights of the big city.

In 1945 the only paved roads in town were the highway and a few blocks of Main Street. I remember blazing hot summer days in that near-desert country when I ran down the sandy streets from Grandmother's house to Aunt Vernie's hovel, racing from shadow to shadow to keep from frying the six-year-old soles of my bare feet. But just as Jim and Curtis never saw the creek in its gloriously wild broken-bridge era, neither can they recall a time when any of the streets in town were unpaved, including the one that now runs past our front door and crosses the creek.

Beside the marshmallow fire that night we four brothers discovered a clear generation gap in our memories of the Key Place. Our childhood experiences of this place, so dear to each of us, were so dissimilar that they might well have happened on different planets. During our earlier cherished retreats to the Robert Lee homeplace, B. and I had mindlessly assumed that our younger siblings treasured the same precious mental images that had been imprinted in our older heads since childhood. Huddled around the fire pit on that brisk October night, we brothers acknowledged what we always should have known—that the memories of young and old were not, and never could be, the same.

Somewhere in his journals that marvelous British curmudgeon G. K. Chesterton wrote, "There are only two kinds of people; those who accept dogma and know it, and those who accept dogma and don't know it." If I may borrow his deft syntax, I would posit as well that there are just two kinds of people—those who are shaped by the generation they live in and know it, and those who are shaped by the generation they live in and don't know it.

In our churches, on our community agency boards, in our classrooms and Internet chatrooms and coffee shop dialogue, we need to keep this inescapable reality clearly in focus. *All of us have been shaped and aimed by the age we live in. We have absorbed the preconceptions of our era, blind spots and all.* Children of the Great Depression will never see the world through the same social and spiritual lenses as will the flower children of the anti-Vietnam days.

One generation is not better than the other. They are just different, in such remarkable ways, and each has insights denied the other. My younger brothers are not inferior to me because their memories lack the wilderness beyond the broken bridge, but in a very true sense my generation possesses something theirs does not.

Long before any of us came to know former President Bill Clinton as a fellow who could not be trusted either with the truth or with White House interns, my soul quaked a bit when I saw his first slate of key advisers. Some of them were brilliant, unquestionably brainier and more capable than their predecessors. Their credentials were impressive. They had been to the right schools and held the right jobs. On paper they looked great.

What bothered me about them was not their credentials or their abilities. What troubled me was their age. To cope with the monumental requirements they would face, they were simply too young. They had not lived through a major war. They had not steered a business through a major economic crisis. They were born after the race riots in Watts and Detroit and Birmingham. They reached puberty after *Roe vs. Wade.*

It was apparent to many of us that this new young team lacked sufficient life experience to assess the consequences of the crucial decisions they soon would have to make. Many Americans shared my fears that this stable of young advisers would serve our president no better than the youth who directed King Rehoboam in the days right after wise Solomon was laid to rest. You may recall that those youthful officials cost the new king most of his kingdom.

With good reasons the presidents of the United States have almost always surrounded themselves with older cabinet members—men and women who have been tested and proved by years of leadership in other arenas. "He who has been faithful over a little shall be given charge over much," Jesus taught, thus describing a principle we ignore at our own peril when we are searching for top leaders in industry, government, academia, or churches.

Designate twenty-year-olds to throw baseballs, tackle half-backs, win marathons, or bring home Olympic gold. Gray hair will be a detriment on a soccer team. Arthritic joints and cataracts will not enhance the competitive edge of your roster in any professional sport. But when you're looking for a man to do the thinking and the strategizing for your team, hire a savvy old codger like Casey Stengel or Don Zimmer to sit on your bench. Get a cagey old fellow like Tom Landry or Vince Lombardi to prowl your sideline. "Been there, done that" may be the rather flip, blunt way of claiming nowadays to know the ropes, but anyone in charge of anything very important needs to be able to say that.

When I look into the cockpit of the 787 I am boarding, I don't want to see a pilot who has been shaving for only half a decade. Give me gray hair every time. Aviation history proves that experience translates into safety—especially in crisis times. Have you noticed that the captains of aircraft carriers and cruise ships always are mature men—well beyond middle age—veterans of the sea who know how quickly one lapse in judgment could scuttle the massively expensive vessels they command?

Several times in recent years the red warning flags have gone up in my heart and the alarm bells have jangled in my head when I have heard that the search committee of a large, proud congregation has decided to call a dynamic young minister whose thirty-year-old vitality made him so much more attractive than the balding candidate who bore the scars of half a century of solid ministry. In more cases than one I have seen these great churches shaken to their roots by pastoral decisions or indiscretions an older and wise minister would not likely have made.

When looking for a new senior minister, some of the fastest-growing churches commit gross age discrimination, actually redlining any pulpit prospect over forty—thereby denying themselves access to the depth of study and the keenness of insight possible only to those who have spent years learning to walk on the pastoral waters. Those churches are so much poorer because of the limits they have imposed upon themselves.

One of Leo Tolstoy's most unforgettable characters in *War and Peace* is the crusty old Russian commander-in-chief, General Kutuzof. That gruff old warhorse had long since passed the age when normal men would have gladly gone to pasture. His political opponents and even his more friendly colleagues characterized him as a dinosaur who had outlived his kind. But Tolstoy attributed to this aging warrior the sort of perception peculiar to those who have been in the trenches for a long time.

"He, with his sixty years' experience, knew how much dependence was to be put on hearsay, knew how prone men who wished anything were to group all the indications in such a way as to conform with their desire, and he knew how . . . they are glad to drop out of sight anything that may seem opposed to it," Tolstoy wrote of him.

Such is the wisdom reserved for those who have lived long and learned well. Does this help us understand why God chose to entrust the leadership of local churches to "elders"?

Little did my parents know how much they would bless our family when they produced a second crop of kids. Having little brothers who are just slightly older than my own offspring has been an important part of my ongoing education. Seeing the evolving world through their eyes has helped me stay more relevant than I probably could have without their aid.

After serving almost twenty years as managing editor of the monthly devotional magazine *The Christian Appeal*, the loss of some of our most significant unpaid volunteer staff caused me to pass the editorial mantle to one of my much younger brothers. I had enjoyed that part of the work on the magazine—planning issues, soliciting articles to flesh out each monthly theme, editing the work of our volunteer writers, laying out each issue, midwifing each month's new birth through the various printing stages, and—at the same time—raising funds to pay the printer and the post office.

The churches I served were gracious in seeing this investment of my time and creative energy as part of their ministry. Not once did any church leader criticize this drain on my time for the local work. When the multiple tasks of the circulation office landed somewhat unexpectedly on my desk, however, it became apparent that my boat was perilously overloaded. So I turned to little brother Curtis as a fellow who shared my love affair with printer's ink and who combined that with writing and editorial skills that were blossoming right at that moment.

Surely the hand of the Lord was in all of this. I look now at the magazine issues we printed in those transitional days and clearly see the imprint of the fresher, younger editorial eyes—eyes attuned far better than mine to the feel and mood of a new generation of readers. I had guided the publication through the monumental changes from linotype galleys and Ludlow headlines on flatbed presses through the first Compugraphic cold-type systems with all the messy cutting and pasting into the earliest days of computer-based layout.

In my tenure we had barely emerged from the Dark Ages of printing, but the technology of the print shop was destined to make light years of progress in that first decade Curtis edited the magazine. Being a closet computer nerd, he embraced the rapid-fire changes with gusto, soon becoming an expert in the use of sophisticated publishing software programs such as QuarkXPress and Adobe Photoshop.

During these past three decades, *The Christian Appeal* has needed my mature hand on the tiller to keep the business end of the operation afloat. God put me where I needed to be, even if I did fuss about the pain of that transition. Not only in the unseen, make-ready operations for each issue but also in the more obvious level of content and graphic appeal, however, the magazine's success and survival depended on having Curtis's younger hand at the ship's wheel.

That night beside the fire pit at the Key Place, if you had challenged us older brothers, B. and me, to evaluate our memories in comparison to those of our younger siblings, our first response likely would have been wrong. We older brothers would have asserted that our recollections of the broken bridge and the jagged path to the wild west bank of the creek made our memories more complete and accurate than Jim's and Curtis's later impressions. They simply came along too late to know the true nature of our beloved creek. B. and I knew the real creek.

Older guys have been asserting such claims of superiority ever since Adam confronted the second generation on the planet. "You guys just don't have any idea what it was like during those first blessed days in Eden," he probably blustered to Cain and Abel around their campfire somewhere east of the Garden. But the truth was that Cain and Abel likely had a clearer perception of their recently cursed world than their father did. Adam kept looking at things through eyes distorted with his regrets. He never got a really clear view of their present real estate because he kept remembering the paradise he lost and could never return to.

Chances are that Jim and Curtis in their later generation may have a more accurate grasp of the Key Place's true state than we in the Medicare set ever can. The young guys see the broad, paved road leading past our door to a sedate, small-town neighborhood. They see what's really there—while we who fancy that we are older and wiser have trouble seeing past the long-gone cul-de-sac and our boyhood footprints in the blistering sand of a long-vanished path. We tend to see what we wish was still there. The younger set see what actually exists today.

Whose vision is better? Does one view trump the other? The answer likely will depend on the age of the person you ask.

Whether viewpoints held by younger generations are superior to those espoused by us older folks is a question for which there may be no definitive answer. But it's a cinch that the two viewpoints *are* different.

Every school day for forty years I have begun my morning with a class full of alert, curious high school students. I tell my teacher friends at this large public high school that I have the best teaching position in all the world. Since the school district doesn't pay me a penny to teach the academic Bible course, they also do not require me to shuffle the reams of paper, attend the endless meetings, and jump through whatever hoop the present generation of legislators has conjured up to harass my longsuffering teacher/ colleagues who are trying to educate the state's children (almost always a variation of some strategy the system tried thirty years ago and long since gave up on). I get to enjoy all the exhilaration of teaching while escaping most of the frustrations of the modern pedagogical system.

During those fun years in the classroom, without doubt the kids have taught me more than I have taught them. They bless me by allowing me to see the world through their eyes. And I cannot deny that they live in a different world than I do.

When I first began teaching the Bible course, I dreamed up what I thought was a fun assignment for my classes. When we came to the book of Judges, I told the kids to pick out a single escapade of one of the judges and write it as though they were newspaper reporters doing the story for the morning paper, headline and all. Those creative, brainy youngsters forty years ago produced some delightful stuff for me.

I have finally faced the reality, however, that my students today cannot handle this seemingly simple assignment. They have no idea what I'm asking them to do because they don't read newspapers. This generation gets its news in sound bytes at 6, or in shorter snatches at the top of each hour on the radio. Or they dabble in snippets of news on the Internet. All of the news they absorb is graphic or aural. When they try writing newspaper stories for me, the result sounds like cue cards for David Letterman.

So I have given up on what used to be a great assignment. It belongs to the Dark Ages of old geezers like me, who can't start a day without newsprint stains on their elbows. Marshall McLuhan turned out to be more right than I wanted him to be when he predicted in his erroneously titled book *The Medium Is the Massage* that we have moved from a world of print to a world of moving graphics as the way to communicate truth.

Almost every Sunday for more than fifty years I have stood in somebody's pulpit to proclaim the Good News of Jesus. Does what the kids have taught me in the classroom have any bearing on how I ought to preach and how we ought to "study" the Bible in churches today? Arguing among ourselves about the merits of the old approach versus the new is pointless. Like wine connoisseurs, those of us with much gray hair will almost always say, "The old is better."

Jesus told us it would be this way. But trying to decide whether old ways surpass new ones ignores the inescapable reality that the new has already eclipsed the old. Whether we like it or not, the way people learn today is the way people learn. If we choose to ignore that reality, we won't change it. We will just make sure that people won't be learning much from us.

Better or worse is not the question. How does it work today? That's the topic we need on the table.

Although the Master was middle-aged by the actuarial charts of his day, he never got too old to appreciate what children can teach us. "Out of the mouth of babes you have brought perfect praise," he noted when the youngsters loudly welcomed him on that first Palm Sunday. "Unless you become like children," he warned, "you can never enter the kingdom of heaven." When people dismissed C. S. Lewis' Chronicles of Narnia as mere "children's stories," the delightful Brit rejoined that the only people who disdain youth are 1) adolescents who are ashamed that they are not yet grown up, and 2) grown-ups who are too stuffy and arrogant to savor the laughter and fun of small children, people who have lost sight of the joy of living.

The generation gap we brothers stumbled into beside the Key Place fire pit that night has beset the transmission of information and truth as long as multiple generations have coexisted. Age-based variations of perception have always presented challenges to the generations on both sides of the gap, but God has always expected his truths to bridge these gaps.

Over and over in the Pentateuch we find the phrase "for generations to come." In Genesis 9:12, for example, God tells Noah, "This is the sign of the covenant I am making between me and you and every living creature with you, a covenant for all generations to come." This clearly implies an expectation that the knowledge of God and his goodness would be communicated from father to son to grandson, jumping the gaps that so often threaten to disrupt the flow of truth.

God expected Jewish fathers to bridge the gap by sharing their love for the Lord and his holy laws with their children continually. "These commandments that I give you today are to be upon your hearts," God commanded. "Impress them on your children" (Deut. 6:6–7).

Only days before his death, the aging apostle Paul told his younger protégé Timothy, "The things you have heard me say [*Generation #1 to #2*] in the presence of many witnesses entrust to reliable men [*Generation #3*] who will also be qualified to teach others [*possibly Generation #4*]" (2 Tim. 2:2).

Thus the Good News of God's grace to us in Jesus is passed successfully across the gaps—generation after generation—an unbroken chain of truth from the Lord Jesus and his apostles reaching to the final inhabitants of Earth who welcome his return.

That night as we sat together in the dark behind the Key Place with the fire pit flames dancing and flickering at our feet, I realized that in my own lifetime six generations of our family have walked on that piece of land, slept in that house, marveled at its sunsets, gazed at the stars, and taken joy in that usually dry creek. From our great-grandfather all the way to our growing host of grandchildren, this place has been our home.

I remember Great-grandfather Shropshire dozing in a metal lawn chair on the front porch with his open Bible precariously perched on his lap. Well into his nineties, hour after hour he used his one good eye to read the Scriptures, although he knew most of them by heart. Hardly a day goes by when I do not see one of my grandchildren poring over the same book, equally mesmerized by its tales of faith and glimmers of truth.

Gap or no gap, the chain of faith continues unbroken.

Chapter 6

My Bedroom

Houses built before air conditioning always had lots of windows. Big windows. Windows that would open wide on every side of the house so you could catch whatever wisp of wind might move on a torrid summer night. This extra ventilation is the most appealing feature of the front bedroom in the Key Place—the bedroom I still call "my bedroom," although I usually sleep in the other one nowadays.

In the beginning this bedroom belonged to my mother and her sister. By the time we grandkids came along, this room on the east corner at the front of the house was known to all of us little guys as Uncle David's bedroom. When his sisters got married and moved away from home, our uncle inherited it as his own private domain, and he slept there until Uncle Sam said greetings and hauled him off to repair the bombers that were pounding Germany and turning the tide of the Second World War.

All of us agreed back then that this bedroom was the best one in the house because it had windows on two sides plus an outside entry with a screen door—lots of openings for fresh air.

By today's standard, both bedrooms in the Key Place are tiny, but this one is the smaller of the two. A double bed with its foot toward the front wall leaves barely enough space for a person to walk between the bedstead and the front window. Positioning that bed almost against the side window leaves between five and six feet of space on the other side, enough for a small chest of drawers parallel to the headboard of the bed.

People who owned no hanging clothes had no need for closets, so my grandparents lived in this house almost half a century without one in either bedroom. When uppity relatives like us showed up with suits and ties and fancy dresses, we could hang up our duds on the wooden bar Uncle David finally devised when he came home on furlough with military uniforms that needed hanging. Triangulated in the corner opposite his bed, this clothes bar barely had space on it for garments on hangers, but all the members of my family were grateful for my uncle's invention whenever we visited my grandparents' house during the decades to come.

In the summer of 1958, this tiny, cramped, cozy, closet-less, but well-ventilated bedroom became "my bedroom." That summer I moved in and lived with my grandparents for three blessed months. The little church where they worshipped invited me to spend the summer between my freshman and sophomore years of college working with them as their preacher.

It was a perfect match. They had never had a preacher, and I had never been one, so neither of us knew enough about such arrangements to know what to expect of the other. They loved me, and I loved them back. What else is there to genuine ministry?

In many ways that was the most glorious summer in my life—the only extended time in my entire life when I lived pretty much by the sun. My grandparents were like most of the other inhabitants of Robert Lee. When it got dark, they went to bed. And when the sun came up, they got up. Being a teenager with wheels, I might have opted for a different schedule, but what would I have done and where could I have gone? They rolled up the streets in that little town about 8:30 every night.

Many a morning during that grand summer I was on the bank of some creek or farm tank (better known as a pond to you Yankees), fishing or rabbit hunting for a glorious hour before I hustled back to the house to swig my granddad's sheepherder coffee and devour the eggs he cooked to death every morning.

In the blindness of my youth it never dawned on me that my grandparents had to stretch their food budget that summer to keep up with the appetite of a growing teenage boy. They never complained, and it was only years later when I was feeding my own brood that I looked back and wondered what my three months of free room and board must have cost them.

From that time on—at least in my eyes—the room where I bunked that summer was "my bedroom."

That summer I struggled hard to keep up with the preaching. Hatching two sermons for every Sunday and another one for Wednesday prayer meetings was just about all a young, dumb kid like me could muster.

Having never employed a minister or any kind of staff, that little church had no study or office—no place for a fellow to hide out with his books and typewriter to conjure up something to preach or teach. I started off trying to study in that tiny bedroom at my grandparents' house. During those first days I crammed a folding card table into the space between my bed and the living room wall, loading that table top with my few books and the portable Royal typewriter my mother had sent south with me for the summer.

The table was adequate. I didn't own enough books yet to fill up a bigger one. The problem with this arrangement was my grandmother's constant and urgent need to be reassured that she was not neglecting me. Every three minutes all day long she would pop into the bedroom door to inquire if I needed anything. She was so proud of what I was doing and so eager to take care of me, but all I really needed from her was an hour or two of uninterrupted silence so I could concentrate on the amateurish sermons I was birthing, with much travail.

Finally I gave up and migrated every morning from that far-too-accessible bedroom down to the study-less small church building. I didn't need the card table there. The small table that on Sundays held the bread and the wine now did double duty. From Monday through Saturday it held the holy Scriptures and all the tools an unprepared youngster like me could marshal to break the bread of life to God's people on the Lord's day.

One Sunday morning during worship just a week or so after I started that summer of preaching, I became uncomfortably aware of a strange little man seated near the door on the very back pew. He had not been there when worship started. I was sure of that. And he vanished before we said Amen. So I didn't get to shake his hand or learn his name. But it was impossible for me to overlook his presence. That old codger stood his walking stick between his knees, propped his chin on his fingers laced atop the walking stick's crook, and stared a hole through me the entire time I preached. I was nervous already, and that old fellow with his intense gaze gave me the willies. This went on for several Sundays.

"Who is that old-timer?" I asked some of the church leaders.

"Oh, that's Grandpa Wallace," some of his family told me, surprised that I didn't know. "We're delighted that he's showing up at church," they beamed. "He hasn't attended for years."

Twenty-eight years to be exact. This old gentleman's sons and grandchildren and great-grandchildren were the core members of the congregation I was serving. By doing a bit of digging, I found out that he once had been an elder of that church. Over a decade before I was born, somebody finally told me, the men of the church gathered one day to pour concrete to double the size of their church building. One brother proposed to do it one way. Elder Wallace was quite sure that this approach would make a mess. The first brother evidently could yell louder. He got his way.

That summer when I came to preach in that enlarged building, the unsightly seam in the bare concrete floor still bore mute testimony that the first brother's construction strategies had indeed been poor ones. Elder Wallace had been right. He knew he was right all along. When the church decided not to follow his good advice that day so many years before my summer there, he stomped off the construction site, fuming that he would never again set foot on that botched-up piece of concrete.

Others involved in that tragic fuss had gone long ago to meet their Maker, but for twenty-eight years Grandpa Wallace kept his promise, until that summer when I came to preach at Robert Lee.

I would have liked to think that he was drawn back through the church doors by news of the smashing sermons being delivered by the church's new young preacher. I knew better than that.

My ego would have liked to believe that he at least was attracted back to the church by the heightened level of activity that accompanied my coming to town that summer. Indeed, we were filling the pews every Lord's day, and many of those who came to worship were members of his own clan who were showing a greatly revived interest in the work of the Lord. But even the church's spurt of vitality was not what drew him back.

Before that summer was over and my fledgling ministry there was completed, Grandpa Wallace brought joy to every heart in our little church when he made his way down the aisle as we sang our traditional invitation hymn one Sunday morning. Few eyes were dry that day when he came home to the church he had walked out on so many years before. It was a heady day for a young preacher, who had done virtually nothing to make it happen.

Late that summer I learned what Paul Harvey would have called "the rest of the story."

During the days of my brief summer ministry, I had a chance to visit with several veteran preachers who had roamed the Robert Lee area, preaching on Sundays and holding summer revivals there long before I was born. I found out that a host of them had made serious efforts to bring Brother Wallace back to the fold, all of them without success. He had left that church mad. He was still mad. He intended to stay mad all of his days. And no preacher was going to convince him to do otherwise.

I was not the only preacher who deserved no credit for bringing this sinner home again. God had a better plan in mind.

During the spring that year, several weeks before I came to preach in Robert Lee, Grandpa Wallace was moseying around in his garden early one morning, inspecting the radishes and exterminating tomato bugs with well-aimed pokes of his walking stick, when his precious six-year-old great-granddaughter (who had obviously been listening to the concerns of her parents and grandparents) looked up at the old man she loved and asked him innocently, "Grandpa, when you are going to get right with God?"

Those were the words God used to touch that untouchable heart, spoken by the only person that old man could hear.

For somebody somewhere, could it be that you are that person?

Sleeping in "my bedroom" during that summer of my pastoral inauguration was blessedly refreshing. I slept solid, sound, undisturbed every night, so I awoke feeling thoroughly rested.

Despite the hype of modern mattress ads telling us that only on their brand of compressed air or scientifically separated spring coils can a person truly find rest, nobody who ever slept on the bed in that bedroom would have credited that mattress as a cause for rest. Several coats of paint bore witness to the age of the metal bed frame. It was ancient. And I doubt that either the old-fashioned open metal springs or the heavy cotton mattress atop them had been replaced in over thirty years. So they were not the reason for the restfulness of that room.

Those of us who have reached Medicare age might be tempted to point out that my nineteen-year-old body—like most healthy young bodies—was still free of the aches and creaks and cramps that afflict us in later life. Looking back at those pain-free years, peering out of the body I live in today, I would not try to deny the truth in such a suggestion. But I'm convinced that my sound, restful slumber in that room could be attributed to another factor.

It would be another decade or so before mercury vapor lights banished the blessed blackness of the night outside those open bedroom windows. And television had not yet taught country people to stay up until midnight, so except for an occasional cross-country truck cruising down the highway a block north of us, we seldom heard the rumble of a vehicle after bedtime.

The street in front of the house still ended in the cul-de-sac that dead-ended at the remains of the flood-ravaged bridge, so we had no traffic. All along the west side of our property the dry creek bed with its thicket of cactus and mesquite walled us off from sparsely settled land beyond the creek. So sleeping in that bedroom was almost like sleeping in a farmhouse far removed from the city.

The quietness and the total darkness of such a setting engulf you in a cocoon. I've heard city folks complain that they can't sleep soundly out on a farm because "it's too quiet." The Key Place back in those pre-citified days was like that—dark and silent.

Today when I sleep in that same old house, however, I opt for the back bedroom that has windows only on one side. "My bedroom"—the front corner one—with windows on two sides is no longer a restful place. Whoever sleeps in that room gets more ventilation, but they pay for it with an invasion of glaring light from the streetlight posted in front of the Smiths' place across the road and with an assault of almost endless traffic noise far into the night.

Fewer windows in the bedroom I now claim as "mine" means less sleep disruption from the light and noise pollution that seem to grow with each passing year.

Even as I complain about these irritants, I recognize that most residents in Robert Lee do what people in big cities do to shut them out. They close all their windows, often doubling the muting effect with storm windows, and they turn on central air conditioning equipment to further mask offending outside noises with a steady inside drone of their own. Heavy draperies on their windows also block out streetlights that might hamper sleep. The nocturnal disturbances that nettle me don't bother them at all.

But I'm convinced that something is wrong with this picture. If you're going to sequester yourself in a man-made environment and block out any hint of God's world outside, why live in a place like Robert Lee? You might as well live in Houston or Manhattan.

Closed up tight like that, you won't have to worry about too much light or noise, but you also will never smell the freshness of just-fallen rain. You'll never hear the palaver of birds excitedly greeting the dawn. You'll never feel the coolness of nighttime breezes filtering through the trees in the last dark hours of the night. You'll miss out on the healthy, gentle wake-up calls of nature as the first rays of morning light begin to soften the darkness and a neighbor's rooster starts begging for more.

Having to give up "my bedroom" in order to get a decent night's sleep still irks me a bit, but I realize that fussing about the world as it is makes about as much sense as complaining about gravity. It's the kind of foolish habit old geezers like me are prone to fall into. Perhaps I should choose instead to give thanks for the two open windows in my present bedroom that still allow me to get a good night's sleep while I stay substantially exposed to the wholesomeness of God's good world outdoors.

Both in my magazine (*The Christian Appeal*) and elsewhere in my newspaper columns and books, I have groused from time to time about the growing light and noise pollution that threaten to rob us of the blessed darkness and restful silence once common to this little town but utterly unknown to those whose days have been spent in larger cities. When I have complained in print, I know that some of my readers probably wrote me off as a crotchety old codger who got up that day in a fussy mood. In fact, a few of them wrote and told me to quit grinching and get a life. They failed to understand my genuine grief at losing something so precious— something they obviously had never known or appreciated.

I hope it's not just the universal, carnal need to say "I told you so," but I did find myself saying a fervent "Amen" as I read an Associated Press report about a whole bunch of folks in Vail, Colorado, who were lamenting the same invasion of civilized racket into their once-remote ski retreat.

Today their Main Street is I-70. Thousands of trucks and RVs and vacation-bound travelers roar through their canyons and mountain passes every day, and the crescendo of traffic noise is forcing people who always have slept with windows open and allowed God to do the air conditioning to start sealing up their homes like big-city folks. And they're sick at heart because of it. No more cool mountain breeze to refresh their slumbers. Replace it with the constant roar and grind of air-handling machinery.

"When you live up here in the mountains, you want to hear the rustling of the creek, not the highway," longtime resident Sybill Navas told the AP reporter. A lot of her neighbors agree. They worry about the eventual effect on tourism and property values. Another Vail resident, Charlene Marquez, said, "If they don't do something soon, they might as well write this town off."

Let me assure you that Robert Lee, Texas, is no Vail, Colorado. Except for the brief run on property thirty years ago when the feds dammed up the Colorado River and temporarily created the E. V. Spence Reservoir, Robert Lee has never been a tourist destination. Which is the main reason guys like me are attracted to it when we're looking for some place to get away from the press of people and the incursion of civilization.

I sympathize with those folks up in Vail. Hearing their concerns gave me a good feeling because they validated my own.

I have been grousing about the slow but inexorable invasion of modern civilization into a sequestered spot—a kind of holy sanctuary—that has somehow managed to remain refreshingly rural and rustic and restful while the rest of the planet opts for the glare of more and brighter lights and for the constant din of more and louder noise.

But you know as well as I do that "my bedroom" in the Key Place is not the only place in today's frenetic world where it is increasingly difficult to find rest or peace. And excessive lumens and decibels are not the main offenders. In this age of broadband Internet and satellite dishes and cell phones and telemarketers and Facebook and YouTube and Twitter, we are bombarded continually with more information than any of us can process— much of it laced with distress and dismay almost certain to unsettle our souls.

Several times a day on most normal days I log on to Fox News or CNN to learn about the latest disaster or the most recent carnage in our world. Within minutes of a riot in Singapore or a terrorist attack in Madrid, I know the gory details. If a plane crashes in Bahrain or a tsunami drowns thousands in Bangladesh, my computer screen instantly informs me of those losses and offers me live video of the devastation in progress. Famines in Ethiopia and bird flu epidemics in China are part of the updated news that inundates us every half hour. Ebola on the other side of the globe becomes my daily focus. And, if I am a Christian with an ounce of compassion—if I am a prosperous American with adequate food and top-notch health care—how can I keep from agonizing about what I should be doing to show mercy to those who are starving and dying at that very hour?

C. S. Lewis may have been right. Without apology he confessed to his friends and colleagues that he seldom read a newspaper or listened to broadcast news. Perhaps because he was an expert in the literature of medieval days, he chose to reclaim in his own life one of the chief luxuries of those long-past days. In the days before air transportation and electronic media, news traveled at camel pace, so its impact on its readers was far less brutal and jarring than it is today.

By the time a person in the sixteenth century read in a London newspaper that a plague had wiped out tens of thousands in

Bombay, the plague had already run its course, all the bodies had been cremated, all the funerals held, and life was proceeding again as near to normal as it ever does in such a place. At this point there was really nothing a Christian halfway around the world could do about the tragedy. Reading news back then did not require immediate, gut-wrenching moral choices. It did not trigger spasms of bitterness or fear or compassion.

Lewis elected to insulate his soul from the daily (and, nowadays, constant) onslaughts of information about matters his ancestors would never have been required to respond to. If they could be good, merciful Christians without such instant knowledge, he assumed that he could too.

Call C. S. Lewis obscurant, or archaic, or nuts, if you want to, but this was his way of addressing one very real source of stress and agitation in our lives today. Just as I yearn for the good old days when my bedroom in the Key Place was dark, many of us are homesick for a time when the crimes and cruelty of earth's nastiest people were not our daily fare.

One summer my wife and I took our oldest son to Ireland. For fifteen heavenly days we bed-and-breakfasted our way across the Emerald Isle, purposely avoiding newspapers or TV reports. For more than two weeks we let somebody else supervise the world while we took some time off from that task. I hated to admit that when we got home and resumed our role as purveyors of daily news and keepers of the planet, the world was actually in better shape than when we had left it.

Looking back, I'm convinced that a large part of the restfulness and delight of our Irish days could be attributed to our conscious decision to disengage ourselves from the ordeal of coming to grips with each day's news. As much as I hate to think that I might be an uninformed citizen in my world, some days I suspect that C. S.

Lewis might have been right. My soul would be far more at peace if I didn't know what new tragedy is unfolding at the top of every hour.

Far more unsettling than the mandates of distant headlines, however, are the strident political debates that seem with each passing year to rage around us with increasing incivility. Ever since Adam was evicted from Eden, mankind has faced hard questions about how best to live. Pain and sweat and toil have been the cursed norm, and the endless discussions about who caused them and how best to cope with them have often become acrimonious.

I can imagine that our first father and his offspring spent many a troubled night beside their campfires hashing over the chain of events that cost them the Garden. Charged with the kind of anger and guilt and regret that seem to accompany all our losses, those fireside confrontations must also have focused on each tribe's touted solution for dealing with the curses Adam brought on both soil and body. Come to think of it, this is pretty much the substance of what we wrangle about today.

In Eden they had no need for a cure for cancer or AIDS or syphilis. Drugs tempted nobody in Eden, because nobody in paradise had any pain or guilt they needed to escape. War was unknown in that perfect age. So was sin. But in those long nights east of Eden the inhabitants of that now-cursed world had more than enough problems and calamities to mull over and fuss about when they found that none of the fixes they proposed worked very well or for long.

Has there ever been an age since then when Earth's inhabitants have not struggled with one another to impose first one solution and then another—whether economic, political, philosophical, or theological—to undo the damning effects of the Fall? And it is this global conversation which seems in this generation to have reached a crescendo pitch that threatens to become intolerable to our ears or our souls.

The growing city noise that now makes it hard to sleep in "my bedroom" at the Key Place is but a mild irritant compared to the rising onslaught of blatantly clashing theories about how to solve the woes of planet Earth. These are some of our age's most raucous assaults on our inner peace.

Several years ago I heard a world-hunger expert discussing his life's work. He could boast that during his career he had developed several hardy strains of grain that were now feeding underdeveloped nations. His efforts brought irrigation to arid lands and abundant poultry to villagers who often had no meat. Because of his efforts, food relief agencies now were feeding hundreds of thousands in malnourished tribes. But, on the eve of this humanitarian's retirement, he had to confess that more people on the globe were starving each day than when he started.

Deep-rooted human needs like this seem to be so intractable, so unfixable, that even the best-spirited people are tempted to throw up their hands at the futility of it all. Behind all the biggest tragedies, of course, are people, whose greed and hate and ignorance inflict massive hurt on whole tribes and nations—Sudanese Muslims intent on wiping out the predominantly Christian southern tribes, Communist state leaders raping the public treasury and bankrupting national businesses while the masses suffer in the resulting penury, Hutus and Tutsis mindlessly bathing Rwanda in blood, or ISIS terrorists and petty warlords in Afghanistan and Pakistan and Iraq whose endless battles for personal wealth and power plunge whole regions of our world into stone-age conditions.

Does this explain why the hungriest people on the globe live on its most fertile soil, why the deadliest terrorists spend the most hours in prayer, why the largest chunk of medical research dollars get spent on the people most likely to continue the behavior that kills them? From every corner of the world the inhumanities being inflicted by man on man scream from newspaper headlines and television screens, effectively banishing peace of mind and serenity of soul from any thinking person.

What should we do when something inside us finally squats under the load and says, "Enough"? What should we do . . .

- When we reach the spot where we say that we can't spend one more day worrying about radical Islamic terrorists committed to a worldwide jihad to wipe out Jews and Americans (whom they mistake for Christians)?
- When we get so weary of the politicians slinging mud and calling each other liars that we begin to lose faith in the only system that has ever offered much in the way of freedom?
- When the in-your-face tactics of homosexual activists make us realize with a sick feeling in our gut that we are leaving our grandchildren a nation where only those who are perverted will have a right to speak freely of their vile beliefs and practices, while the majority will be branded hateful and criminal if they speak their own convictions on these matters or dare to read aloud what God says on the subject?
- When we get caught in the passionate rhetoric of those who would move heaven and earth to defend whales and timber wolves and bald eagles but are equally ardent to defend the legal right to exterminate humans who are infirm or unborn?
- When we find our own strong prolife beliefs discredited by some fruity fanatic who decides to end the baby killing by doing some killing of his own?

What do we do when the bitter wrangling over seemingly unsolvable issues rages on and on, so that our souls no longer can rest?

Sometimes it's tempting to follow Thoreau to Walden Pond and pretend that the real world with its jangling, jarring controversies doesn't exist. Sometimes, when the spiritual static gets too crackly to endure, we understand what drove those ancient Essenes to pack up their families and move out into the Judean desert to live in total isolation from governments and schools and religious hierarchies.

Wouldn't it be grand some days just to drop out of the whole mess—to retreat to some deserted South Sea island and let the world take care of its own imponderables from now on?

But Paul Harvey was right when he used to say, "You can run, but you can't hide." Not if you have an ounce of mercy or compassion or thoughtfulness in you. Not if you're hooked up with a sense of responsibility and love for your fellowman.

The Scriptures tell us that we fulfill everything God tries to tell us in his laws when we bear one another's burdens. Part of doing that surely involves coming to grips with the critical issues that threaten the survival and quality of life of us all. Certainly, though, there must be some way for us to keep from burning our hands and searing our souls when we take hold of the hottest topics that polarize our generation.

Famous authors C. S. Lewis and J. R. R. Tolkien had a lesser-known writer friend named Charles Williams. Together they became the most famous members of a fellowship of friends which these sharp-witted penmen dubbed "the Inklings." The lesser-known member of this grand trio may have put his finger on one answer to my concerns here when he wrote, "Holy anger is a very dangerous thing indeed for anyone who isn't a saint to play with."

Even in the most ancient days people felt compelled to struggle with issues so grave that they often described themselves as wrestling with the gods. The struggle is nothing new. But the intensity of emotional heat—especially the quickness and fierceness of the anger involved—does appear to be a new ingredient in today's public discourse. The civility that once characterized even the verbal exchanges of sworn enemies has vanished for the most part, and spokesmen on every hand—in pulpits, on the political dais, and the TV anchor desk—adopt the tone of righteous indignation. And we who get drawn into their debates find ourselves seething inwardly with wrath, for which we seldom can identify a legitimate target.

Williams was right. "Holy anger" poses a dire threat to those of us who are mere mortals. Listen to an hour of almost any radio talk show or eavesdrop on just about any coffee klatch at the local donut shop and you will come away convinced that such anger is in abundant over-supply today. All around us people are irate, upset, fearful, and stressed out about things they are just as powerless to modify as I am to eliminate the nocturnal disturbances that invade the open windows here at this old house.

The last time I slipped down to Robert Lee to spend a week reading and studying at the Key Place, my open-window bedroom habits exposed me to a new phenomenon. Commercial trash dumpsters behind the various businesses in the town are emptied a couple of times a week. I did not know that, since my last visit to town, a new trash company from some nearby city had assumed this duty. On their schedule of area towns to be serviced, Robert Lee drew the 5 A.M. slot.

Right when I was snoozing most soundly, the crash-bang-whump of a nearby dumpster being slam-dunked by a garbage truck shattered my slumber. From one end of the small town to the other, the roar and rumble and racket of the same process was repeated, often punctuated with the shrill beep-beep-beep of the trash truck's back-up horn and the grinding of the truck's mechanism as it compacted its new load. Half an hour of this cacophony banished sleep for anybody in the town—at least if their windows were wide open like mine. Two mornings a week now we replay this travesty.

So much for the quiet little town where a fellow can get away from it all.

Chapter 7

The Landfill

For almost half a century my grandfather waged a one-man war against the erosion that threatened to reduce his usable property. Our side of the creek bank slowly crumbled and washed away back in the years when floodwaters swelled and raged past his place. Before soil conservation became a high priority for farmers and other rural landowners, Granddaddy tried his own innovative methods to stop the vagrant weather from stealing his precious land.

EPA rules today would curtail such practices, but before Uncle Sam showed up to cure our problems with all his infinite wisdom, on virtually every farm and ranch in the nation the owner had his own private landfill where his family dumped their household garbage along with any refuse generated by their agricultural endeavors. And most of those home-owned trash dumps served the same purpose my grandfather's did. Dumping trash in a draw helped curb the runoff rainwater that carried precious topsoil into creeks and rivers below.

The amazing thing about our private landfill was its location right in town. On our heavily wooded creek with no neighbors on the opposite side during those early days, my grandparents could heave their household garbage over the creek bank without offending a soul. I doubt that three people outside our extended family even knew they did it, and those who did would have considered it a wise land-management tactic.

We grandkids first became aware of Granddaddy's conservation goals when we got big enough to haul the kitchen trash from the house to the creek. He went with us the first few times, clearly explaining to us his strategies for preserving the creek bank and thereby enlisting us in his anti-erosion war.

Half a century before recycling became the rage, our family separated our trash. Combustible items went into one can, to be burned every morning in the barrel in the back patch. Non-combustibles to be deposited on the fragile red dirt along the steepest part of the vanishing creek bank filled another can. Each trash can full of bottles and cans thus became our family's united effort to preserve our property. By the time I was a teenager I had long before lost count of the trips I had made to empty Grandmother's trash can and to save the bank of our creek.

By that time, however, more serious conservation efforts upstream had quelled the tendency of the creek to flood. Even in the heaviest rains we seldom saw water more than two or three feet deep in the creek anymore, and it stayed down in the center channel where it posed no threat to the banks we were working so hard to protect. Little by little vegetation began to root in the soil that once was washing away at an alarming rate.

Then, to the amazement of all the older residents of the area, Americans got caught up in the bottle-collecting craze, and to our delight we discovered that our old family landfill had suddenly become a veritable mine of treasures. At one time or another during the '60s I watched just about every one of my relatives on the Key side of the clan delving into the family landfill on our creek bank, hoping to unearth some of the rare bottles we had discarded there in the decades past. Marketers about that time were discovering the miracle of plastic packaging, and it dawned on collectors that the glass bottles of the first half of the century were quickly becoming extinct. So the hunt was on all over the nation.

Do you remember when Phillips' Milk of Magnesia came in dark blue bottles with the red, white, and blue labels? My grandparents always had a bottle or two on hand, so the creek bank was littered with them. Grandmother used some sort of salve that came in four-inch-tall bottles that were a soft Hereford brown, about twice as wide as they were thick, with gentle curves on the vertical corners.

Mercurochrome was a household staple before medics discovered that it wouldn't kill germs. Feeling it sting on a scrape or cut and seeing its red stains on our skin at least made us think we were properly doctored, so we got well anyway. It came in tiny dark brown bottles between two and three inches tall, with a clear-glass applicator stick attached to the inside of the cap. With so many grandkids on the place, all of us constantly stubbing toes and scraping knees, we used buckets of it, so those bottles were plentiful.

Grandmother didn't use much makeup, but I remember that the cold cream and the few cosmetics she did indulge in came in small but heavy-bottomed hockey-puck-shaped jars. With fancy metal lids almost as wide as the footprint of the jars, most of them were hollowed out with smooth, shallow, half-moon indentions inside their dense bottoms. They were weighted to make them feel like they held far more of the product than they really did. Lying buried in the creek bank soil, most of the ornate metal lids rusted away through the years, but the jars themselves were almost indestructible, so we found a lot of them as we scavenged for antique glass.

The Calumet baking powder cans were not glass, of course, but since Calumet had started packaging their product in cardboard "cans," the old metal ones also became prizes worth finding in a bottle dig. The Indian-chief logo on the cans would outrage the politically correct today, but back then before everybody and his cousin decided to feel discriminated against, nobody thought anything about it.

During the roll-your-own-cigarette years, most of Granddaddy's tobacco came in the pocket-sized cloth sack with the yellow twine drawstrings and cardboard tags that dangled out of the shirt pocket of every cowpuncher in West Texas. But for a period back in World War II days, for some reason Granddaddy switched to Prince Albert in the flat, bright red, flip-top metal cans. Prince Albert must have used good paint, because twenty years later some of those long-buried cans were still intact during the bottle-digging days.

If anybody in the 1940s had tried to tell us that two decades later our family would be excitedly excavating our ancestral garbage, we would have declared that they were nuts. Nobody could have convinced us back then that we should be safely storing our day-to-day trash as an investment in the future. No way. But there we were during those naïve JFK days rooting in the family garbage dump like a pack of hungry squirrels digging for long-buried nuts, squealing like magpies when one of us chanced upon an empty, mud-stained bottle we had earlier discarded as worthless junk.

Treasures do tend to lurk in the most unexpected places, don't they? I recall C. S. Lewis's comment about George MacDonald's writing. "Some of his best things are hidden in his dullest books," Lewis opined. It's that way in our own preaching and our teaching.

Some of the dullest sermons contain the keenest insights. Some of our most pedestrian teachers have imparted lessons to us that have lasted the longest. True value so often tends to hide in disguise at the moment, invisible except to hindsight.

Getting farther away—either geographically or chronologically—from whatever we are overlooking does seem to improve our ability to see it. It took two decades or more before we could see empty liniment bottles and Del Monte pickle jars as rare heirlooms worth searching for and saving.

So it is that with each passing year our physical eyesight wanes but our spiritual vision improves, at least for most of us. That grand expositor of Scripture, Warren Wiersbe, testified as he approached his middle years that this certainly was true in his case. He said, "I am not as critical as I used to be, not because my standards are lower, but because my sight is clearer." Then he explained, "What I thought were blemishes in others have turned out to be scars."

I now recall those creek-bank digging days and wonder what there is about us humans that so often makes us value something only after we have thrown it away. Having painstakingly created the crown jewel of modern radio broadcasting, why couldn't a sharp fellow like Garrison Keillor see what a mistake it was to close up shop, turn off the lights, and move off to Denmark where nobody had ever heard of Lake Wobegon? Somewhere he explained that he quit because of "sheer exhaustion." Only when his unequalled show was gone did he realize what he had buried.

I wonder if the creator of the Calvin and Hobbes comic strip now wakes up to pangs of regret when he realizes that he walked away from the kind of success most artists and writers would almost kill to attain. Did the daily drudgery of drawing the strip and the inexorable deadlines for the chore temporarily blind him to the worth of what he had earned the right to do? Maybe not.

But I can't keep from wondering if he gave up more than he knew at the moment. Just as my doctor friend did when he traded in the wife of his youth for one who was half her age. He loves his present wife and treats her royally, but I wonder what he thinks while he sits wistfully on the sidelines and watches at a distance while his children by his first mate graduate from school and get married and produce grandchildren. Does he realize now—too late—that he threw away what mattered far more than he imagined at the time?

With some hard work our family could recover the bottles we had discarded in the creek, but far too many of life's most precious discards are lost to us forever. Like old Esau who lived to mourn the time when he so lightly surrendered his birthright, we may look back with delayed appreciation for blessings we earlier scorned, and all our bitter tears will not undo foolish decisions made in the heat of passion or anger or youthful whimsy.

Some of our relatives were just mildly curious about the treasures embedded in the creek bank. They would wander out to the creek on a cool day and kick at a clod or scratch the surface with shoe sole, halfheartedly bending to extract any item thus exhumed. Once in a while one of these barely interested folks would walk away with a rare find, but the real treasures, as in most of life's endeavors, belonged to those who paid for them with sweat and grime.

Some of the cousins who lived nearer to the trove than I did got conscripted into spending some long, arduous days with their mothers, spading and sifting the sandy red soil on that creek bank. When we would come to visit the grandparents, I enjoyed surveying the relatives' recent finds. Bottles of every imaginable color, shape, and size—long ago discarded and forgotten—began to reappear on the window sills and whatnot shelves in the Key Place and in the homes of my aunts and uncles. During those years every visit gave us a chance to hear the latest excited tale about some unexpected bonanza from the bowels of our creek-bank trash heap.

Then, as quickly as the craze ignited, digging for bottles lost its charm. I suspect the market for antique glass got glutted if every rural family duplicated what ours did, so those shelves and cabinets full of high-priced recovered refuse sat there collecting dust, slowly losing momentary value, little by little devolving back into trash again.

The only thing wrong with this economic assessment is my gnawing awareness that not once in those bottle-collecting days did I see a member of our family or anybody else's family ever sell one of those priceless bottles. I guess the market sagged simply because all of us knew how many houses in counties all across America were laden to the gills, bursting with bottles and all sorts of landfill glass—more than enough to wipe out the market if anybody ever did decide to part with any of it.

It seems ironic to me that my grandfather's unstinting battle to slow the erosion of his creek bank suffered its worst single setback precisely because of the strategy he implemented to preserve the loose soil. Nothing—not wind or rain or floods or freezes—loosened as much of that precious creek-bank dirt as did the decade of bottle digging by our clan. The very waste he strewed there to shore up the land attracted shovels and spades and forks and rakes that loosened the earth and left it more vulnerable than ever before to the vagrant elements. His chosen cure actually wound up aggravating his problem.

To make matters even worse, my grandfather's other method for saving his land turned out to be even more disastrous. In this case, the cure without doubt was worse than the disease.

All over Coke County today you can spot stands of bamboo cane fanning high above the creek beds, mute evidence of the ill-conceived "bamboo fix" for the county's erosion problems. At the time when it was utilized, the concept seemed brilliant. Bamboo spreads like gossip. It is almost indestructible. And, demanding surprisingly little moisture, it seems to be perfectly suited for semi-arid country like that part of West Texas, where month after scorching summer month often passes with ovenlike heat and hardly a dribble of rain.

At some time not long after the record-setting droughts in the late 1950s, the county extension agent began offering free bamboo plants to every landowner with a creek bed, touting this exotic plant as God's answer to erosion in Coke County. My grandfather bought the agent's convincing spiel. Finally he had found a more effective weapon than household trash to shore up the soil and solidify the creek bank that had threatened to vanish from beneath the cedar fence posts along the west edge of the chicken patch.

Within two or three years, towering bamboo sprouts filled the bed of the mostly dry creek. It never seemed to occur to anyone that the much-feared floods of decades past no longer ran high enough or hard enough in our creek to endanger its banks. Diversions upstream had put an end to the wild water. So the bamboo cure was not needed. Granddaddy and the extension agent locked that barn door after the cow had already escaped. And, as so often happens in our world, the treatment they prescribed turned out to be far worse than the malady.

Science is replete with illustrations of this sort of quick-fix-gone-wrong. Park rangers and wildlife experts were so pleased with themselves when they discovered that Chinese carp would uproot moss and lake-bottom vegetation and save fortunes spent each year to dredge and reclaim silted lakes. Somehow it didn't dawn on them that this large, voracious fish would also hog the food supply and soon take over any habitat where it was introduced. Only too late did the same experts realize that this fish is an insufferable pest nobody knows how to get rid of.

So it is with the bamboo that thrives to this day in our creek bed and in dozens of others across the county. You can burn it, grub it, mow it, poison it, and it will thank you by emerging from the earth the next season with lusher leaves and taller sprouts. Like trumpet vine and kudzu and a host of other Asian plants not intended for our hemisphere, bamboo is forever.

Older is not always wiser. It doesn't always work out that way. All of us know some goofy old geezers. But one part of wisdom that can only be gained by longevity belongs to those of us who have lived long enough to recognize reruns of fixes that did not work the first time—whether addressed to the woes of society, government, schools, or the church. We can also point to some colossal "cures"—in actual fact, super-fiascos—that have caused far more damage than the ills they were designed to correct.

If we Americans had it to do over again, for example, how many of us would vote for a national income tax? Have you checked the federal tax codes lately to see how many pages it takes to explain the explanations of the explanations? IRS bureaucrats add several inches to the books each year, with each legally mandated paper reduction and simplification multiplying the system's confusion. Untangling the matted bamboo roots in my Key Place creek bottom would be a simple task compared to the assignment of making sense of America's tax code. Even such root-jarring jolts to our nation as Pearl Harbor and 9/11 have left the income tax system unscathed. Once you breathe into it the breath of life, income tax is forever.

Likewise the grandiose proposals generated to fix America's methods of education. And the ever-lengthening list of governmental regulations that include the word *environmental.* And all the well-meaning but often counterproductive remedies proposed under the auspices of alphabet agencies and acts such as OSHA, ADA, DHS, and OEO.

You know how it works. Rules made to protect the public from unscrupulous buggy whip manufacturers not only outlive that menace but three generations later some government bean-counter with nothing better to do makes it his main priority to enforce those rules with mindless zeal on the manufacturers of space shuttle accelerators. Like the bamboo in my creek, rules made by any governmental agency seem to be forever.

Jesus said something along this line. "Heaven and earth shall pass away," he predicted, "but my words shall not pass away." Nor, he might well have added, shall the customs, procedures, rituals, habits, or rules of any congregation of his people.

In virtually every Christian denomination there seems to be an unwritten but unbreakable mandate that anything done the same way three times in a row becomes, de facto, an unchangeable, eternal, incredibly important norm that can be altered even slightly only if you're willing to risk the fires of hell and the wrath of God and the ire of the deacons (or, at least, their wives). Church people, rooted and grounded in their customs, make it clear to any person brash enough to challenge them: the one unforgivable sin in just about anybody's church is *Change*.

Change your Sunday morning service time and listen to the natives howl.

Change the kind of songs you sing and the decibels of complaint will treble.

Rearrange the order of rituals in the service and some members almost certainly will threaten revolution.

Add a contemporary service and loud wailing will begin, often punctuated by the footsteps of traditional folks leaving.

Go back six months later to a single service like the only one you used to offer and the other half of the flock will threaten to depart.

What most of them are protesting will not be the kind of service proposed. They will be outraged because you had the temerity to suggest that they should *c-h-a-n-g-e*.

I think it was my colleague Dr. Leroy Lawson who shared with me the anonymous little ditty which says,

> *Our fathers have been churchmen*
> *A thousand years or so,*
> *And to every new proposal*
> *They have always chanted "No!"*

Churches, schools, governments, and clubs of every sort have this much in common: we sanctify our rules and rituals and traditions, investing them with lamentable immortality long after the death of the problems they were invented to solve.

Like my grandfather's marvelous bamboo.

"If you don't want your spineless prickly pear hacked down, you'd better call the mayor's office immediately," my Robert Lee cousin, Joe David, alerted me by long distance one afternoon.

A bus full of convicts from a nearby prison had emptied its load of miscreants into my precious creek, armed with hoes, scythes, rakes, mowers, loppers, and saws. At the invitation of the city fathers they had come to clear the brush, fell the trees, hack down the weeds, and haul away the trash—in other words, to remove the creek-bed wilderness I had so carefully nurtured by neglect.

Evidently some of the neighbors west of the creek did not share my immense pleasure in the out-in-the-country atmosphere provided by our creek's wildness. They preferred the in-town, manicured look of a park. So they had enlisted the mayor's sympathies, and he had responded with a busload of able-bodied free labor. A small army of convicts was cleaning up my marvelously overgrown creek.

A quick call to the mayor—a lifelong friend to me and my family—secured his promise that the immense spineless prickly pear on the creek bank not far north of the road would be spared. But in the spirit of neighborliness, and out of recognition that the tangle of dry weeds and shrubs and brush in the creek bed were in fact becoming a formidable fire hazard to all of us who lived nearby, I gave the mayor my approval for his band of prisoners to clean out my part of the creek.

At least two dozen strong men worked hard at the job for two days. By far their toughest enemy turned out to be my grandfather's hearty bamboo. When the convicts were done, huge piles of it, each of them taller than a man's head, were strung all along the creek bed, waiting the prison gang's promised return to remove it. For the first time in a decade I could see my neighbor's house across the creek.

It seemed strange and unsettling—almost exhibitionistic—to be so exposed. For most of my days the Key Place has enjoyed the seclusion provided by that brush in that creek. But I am glad to report that any discomfiture caused by the new openness was short-lived. Within a month or so, the ubiquitous bamboo began to return, thicker and taller than before. By summer's end the neighbors on the west were back where they are supposed to be— discreetly hidden behind the bamboo curtain in the creek.

That's the problem with problems: they don't look like problems when somebody dreams them up.

Back in the late 1920s, Pop Warner's love for kids and his concern for the growing delinquency problems involving big-city juveniles caused him to sponsor neighborhood football leagues to occupy idle youth. Thus, without realizing it at the time, he created the first organized youth sports league in America—the Pop Warner Football League. Close behind came Little League in 1939, and then the Babe Ruth League and the YMCA leagues and an endless proliferation of other community sports organizations for kids.

But things have changed drastically since those programs were hatched. Is anybody in America in the early decades of the twenty-first century worried about kids being idle? My grandkids are so busy playing so many kinds of ball and trying to master various musical instruments that they don't have time to live. Just like most of yours, I suspect.

U. S. News reported that in the past twenty years structured sports time has doubled for our kids. That means, of course, that unstructured sports time—the fun time—has been cut in half. And the average family with two or more kids simply cannot run fast enough to keep up with their associates' manic obsession with signing up their six- and seven-year-old youngsters in the futile chase of college sports scholarships and professional fortunes.

Two decades ago I began seeing families leaving church before the Sunday morning benediction, hurrying to get their kids fed and properly clad in time for the new soccer league games. Today in virtually every church across the nation a host of families simply aren't there for worship on lots of Sundays because they have ferried their sons and daughters to travel-team games. Repeatedly, I hear couples moaning because the father had to haul one child east while

Mama chauffeured another child west to weekend games up to four hundred miles from their front door—with resulting disruption to their family budgets for time, money, and spiritual pursuits.

Leisure time for such families is extinct. For too many families today, youth sports programs are stealing everything a family ought to be, and the problem seems to grow more damaging with each passing year.

I realize that what I have just written will not be popular. It will sound like social heresy to those who have sold their souls to the all-consuming effort to have their children involved in life-building, wholesome school and community activities.

Part of the problem in many cases lies with parents whose own carnal, materialistic goals for their children seek the wealth and status possible to top-level athletes in our time (a goal that is less realistic than winning a state lottery). But much of the blame must rest with the organizers of youth activities on every level.

School bands and choirs and sports teams used to be fun activities that were extracurricular—in other words, neat additions to a school's academic offerings. In today's world, however, almost every band director, drama teacher, journalism sponsor, or tiddlywinks coach demands total commitment from any participating student, often to the exclusion of any other worthwhile character-building activities. And outside of school, most youth sports coaches demand practices or games five and six nights a week and often on weekends as well, leaving no time for church, family, work, or normal juvenile goofing off.

So parents are left to choose between two evils. Either they can refuse to let their children participate in any school or community programs, thus cutting them off from the fun and enrichment of music, sports, drama, and similar activities. Or—as most do today—they can opt for the benefits of involvement and find that they have just surrendered any hope of family togetherness or of any leisure time for anybody in the home, whether young or old.

At some point on this road to ruin, somebody somewhere needs to stand up and say, "Enough!" Somebody needs to reintroduce sanity and moderation into the youth activity mix. But such a message will not likely be applauded by many people today.

In one of his novels James Michener observed, "An age is called Dark not because the light fails to shine, but because people refuse to see it." A generation of people who find their ultimate fulfillment and greatest joy in competing and winning in sports events will not likely be quick to see the dangers inherent in such an obsession.

From whence came this ruinous rat race? From the holy desire to keep idle, unsupervised kids from getting into trouble. How do we repair this growing national disaster? If you figure out how, then please come tell me how to get rid of the bamboo in my creek. One project is just about as doable as the other.

Chapter 8

The Dying Trees

As soon as I got my meager luggage unloaded, got the water turned on, the water heater refilled, and the power switched on for the house, I ambled around the perimeter of the Key Place property, making my customary inspection to see what kind of varmints or blights or bugs had invaded the place in our absence. I was sorry to see that down beside the creek during the winter we lost two more trees.

Trees are precious in Coke County. Rainfall maps call this part of the world semi-arid. Almost desert. With so little rain and so much heat, only the toughest trees survive.

Early this morning, wondering why those apparently healthy trees had died, I returned to the high bank of the now-dry creek that borders our place on the west. Last year's cane bristled tall, dry, and brown from the creek bed, remnants of the out-of-control bamboo introduced decades ago.

Through the waving bamboo heads I could see the two locust trees, standing on the rim of the creek, stark and leafless against the surrounding sea of green. During the winter the always dark locust bark had turned black. Now the bark is scaling off like slabs of decaying skin, leaving leprous splotches on the dead trunks of the trees—the latest casualties to an army of wood borers that in recent decades has decimated the larger trees on the west side of our property.

I'll miss those trees. They were part of an intentional thicket—a welcomed wilderness—that preserves the illusion that our grandparents' place is still out in the country, like it was when we were kids. The small town has slowly, inexorably, absorbed our acreage. We, who come only occasionally, try futilely to preserve the rural feel—with the original stock pens and the weathered shed now visibly deteriorating out back, and the creek bed full of critters desperately holding the encroaching town at bay. The death of the locust trees lets me know that we are losing the battle.

The truth is that all of us are. We spend our entire lives resisting change, trying to keep things like they used to be—like we thoughtlessly feel they ought to be. And everything just keeps changing.

Despite the wisdom we spout at the coffee shop—

Despite the too-simple solutions espoused each day on talk radio—

Despite the mandates of governments and the pontifications of churches—

Despite our own personal prejudices and our obstinate refusal to change our own ways—

Despite all of this, the world around us just keeps changing, and almost without our knowing it, the changes change us, too.

Remember Archie Bunker? Most of that old show's humor erupted from Archie's adamant resistance to change. But after fuming and fussing and pitching a fit, Archie usually relented and accepted the inevitable. He changed. Just as we do.

Changing God's System

Change comes hardest for us, of course, when we're convinced that the status quo is "the way God intends for things to be."

During my father's lifetime mankind moved from covered wagons to space shuttles. For the most part, he adapted to those huge changes with remarkable dexterity of soul. In the final week of his life he was trying to learn to send email. But some changes were not so easy for him to accommodate. No more loving and gentle spirit ever existed than my dad, but he was, like all of us, a creature of his own age.

A few months before he died just a week short of 87, he confided in me with the utmost seriousness that he thought the biggest political mistake during his lifetime was allowing women to vote. Out of concern for his ongoing ministry, I cautioned him, "Dad, don't you ever say that out loud to anybody else." But I could not miss the reality that, well over half a century after it happened, my father was still resisting that change. Not because he was a woman-hating, power-hungry, macho galoot, but because he was afraid we had tampered with God's divine order for society.

If we give God credit as the originator of our peculiar ways, it stands to reason that we will be slow to change them, doesn't it? In pre-World War II days, my grandparents and most of their contemporaries were convinced that God meant for women to wear their hair long. Only Hollywood hussies "bobbed" their hair. Both of my godly grandmothers were crestfallen when my little sister showed up in 1946 with short hair. The change troubled them because they thought God was displeased.

The bulk of Protestant Americans until recent times erroneously identified Sunday as the biblical Sabbath, so they rigorously applied many of the Jewish restrictions to activities on the Lord's day. In his delightful little book about his growing-up years in the

Slabtown section of Montezuma, Iowa, my dear friend Leo Miller told how his godly parents and the equally faithful parents of his next-door cousins frowned on such worldly activities as playing softball on Sunday afternoons. After all, it was the Sabbath.

Especially in the Southern Bible Belt states, blue laws were common. Bars closed. Businesses closed. Sport activities were taboo. Engaging in any sort of manual labor on Sunday would earn you an indignant frown from your righteous neighbors. And those customs were slow to change because in the minds of so many Christians they were based on the Fourth Commandment. They were convinced that the rules reflected God's will.

Remember when Americans were in a tizzy because John Kennedy was a Catholic?

Remember when Nelson Rockefeller's nomination as vice president almost got scuttled because he had been divorced?

Remember when most Southern pastors quoted Scriptures to prove that blacks were an inferior race consigned by God to a subservient role?

Changes come painfully and tumultuously for any cultural norms deemed to be divinely sanctioned. Our resistance to such changes proves the truth of the prophet's words, "Zeal for thy house hath consumed us."

Changes We Don't Notice

Changes are inevitable, of course. Could it be that the ones most likely to alienate us from God are the ones we don't resist because we don't even know they are occurring? These changes are subtle, like the gradual taming of the wild creek bed beside my grandparents' old homeplace. With each passing season a few more bushes wither, another tree gives up the ghost, another streetlight robs us of the blessed rural darkness, and before we know it our beloved creek bed will become a city park.

Looking back over decades now long past, in our churches we can see the effect of these slow, indiscernible shifts. Some of us remember when "church" was the only show in town. Especially in the summertime before high school football busted out in every Texas town. Three-week summer revivals were the norm. Every Sunday afternoon we joined folks from miles around for a "singing" at some area congregation. Long before volunteering got touted as the civic thing to do, all of us just pitched in to do whatever had to be done at the church. Whenever the church doors were open, most of us were there.

Then, with the wisdom one learns to expect from government, some folks in high places decided that it ought to be against the law for kids to hold paying jobs, so in communities all across the land we scrambled to set up sports programs so our idled kids would have something to do. At the same time school programs branched out far beyond the traditional three Rs to include competitive learning experiences in everything from shorthand to piccolo playing. And all of it seemed beneficial at the moment. None of these incremental changes appeared to oppose religion or to encourage immorality, so none of us protested. In fact, most of us applauded and participated.

Today, in our overcommitted age, churches struggle to get meager slices of time from families strapped with unmanageable calendars. Like the rugged wildness of our cherished Key Place creek, the time when churches got the bulk of our energy and talent vanished without our knowing when or how.

The subtle changes that sneak up on us are the ones that do the most damage. In my more pensive moments I find myself wondering, for example, how much my own attitudes and lifestyle have morphed over the years, leaving less room for Jesus and more provision for my own comfort and desires.

A decade ago I sat in the bluebonnet patch beside our Robert Lee creek, being as still as I possibly could be, and in the growing darkness after dusk I watched the critters emerge from the brush beyond the rusty barbed wire fence along the creek. Before long in my flashlight's beam I caught the bright eyes of a possum. He ambled along the creek bank, apparently not spooked by my presence.

Half an hour passed as darkness deepened, and then that skunk I told you about earlier sneaked up on me. Suddenly I was startled by a movement right beside me. In my peripheral vision, in the now-bright moonlight, I had picked up the sweeping movement of the white stripe on a bushy tail. I froze. While I held my breath, the biggest skunk I ever saw ambled past me, his proud tail held high. One wrong move, one cough or sneeze, and I knew he would douse me. He prowled around our patch for several minutes and then scurried, unruffled, back through the brush into the creek bed.

Bobcats used to come up from the creek and prowl the fence row behind our bird feeder. On a few rare occasions we even spotted a deer ambling down the dry creek bed. As I write this, though, it dawns on me that several years have passed now since I've seen any critter except a cottontail rabbit emerge from our creek. Bit by bit the habitat has changed too much for many of them to call it home.

What about the habitat of my heart? Has it been slowly evolving to make it more habitable for me and less for my Lord? Over sixty-five years ago I confessed Jesus as God's Son, my Savior, my Lord. This allegiance has not consciously changed. But it's the unconscious changes that worry me. I'm concerned about the changes I have made without even realizing it during the decades now past.

Long ago I was a naïve fledgling preacher, on fire for the Lord and eager to win the world for him. Today I am the mature professional, far more confident in my pastoral skills but also much wiser in assessing my own limitations. This sounds good. Unless it means that I've simply grown tired and jaded, content now to attempt less, accomplish less, offer less to Jesus.

Although most of us in ministry claim to believe in grace, far too many of us measure ourselves and our success by our works— by what we do. Few heresies are easier to embrace whether you're in ministry or out of it, because it is so much easier to *do* than to *be*.

On every hand I hear people lamenting that they are busier, running faster, working harder than ever before. I know this certainly describes me. As the pace of our lives keeps ratcheting up one tiny notch at a time, is the quality of our lives enhanced? Does being frenetic and frazzled make you a better mother? Or me a better minister?

One reason I retreat to my now-waterless creek is to get out of life's fast lane long enough to let my harried soul catch up. Madeleine L'Engle, whose words on paper almost always bless my soul, writes about how important it is for all of us to "listen to the silence." This is one of the few places on earth where I can still do that. Could this be why Jesus suggested closets for praying? Every other place in my world is wired for sound and filled with duties that require me to be *doing*, instead of listening or *being*.

Accepting the Inevitable

On one level our lifelong resistance to change is irrational. All of us know it.

The locust trees beside our creek bed are not the only trees we've lost on the family homeplace. A large mulberry tree used to stand in the middle of the largest stock pen, its spreading limbs often draped with little boys tormenting the goats and calves below. It froze, or died of thirst. I forget now. Whatever happened to it, it's gone. Closer to the house, Grandmother pampered a large Vitex tree. When my oldest siblings and I were kids, it was our favorite climbing tree. It also died.

A decade before I buried him, I remember my Uncle Fred waddling on permanently injured legs through our west patch to inspect two large old mesquite trees that had died during the previous winter. We wondered why. When he chainsawed them down, we saw where the borers had hollowed out their hearts. Half a century it took for them to grow tall, and just one season for a bug to lay them low.

My grandfather spent the same half century rooting, planting, and grafting pecan trees for the orchard. A decade after he died, my brothers and I killed his hardiest tree. Unintentionally, of course. Only after we hooked up the old house to the city sewer line did we discover that the feeder lines of the ancient septic tank had irrigated that tree. Robbed of its nutrients in that arid land, it soon shriveled. Last winter in my fireplace I burned the last chunks of it.

A catalog of the trees we have lost through the decades is not unlike a list of the generations who have loved this cherished piece of land and then left it forever. Expecting either the trees or the people who planted them to be permanent is folly. They weren't. We aren't. As Isaac Watts's old song says, *"Time, like an ever-rolling stream / Bears all its sons away."*

The two dead locust trees stand today as silent sentinels on the creek bank, reminders that nothing stays the same for long in this world. When I come back, I'll bring my chainsaw and give them back to the earth.

Eternal God, the same yesterday, today, and forever,
You never change.
The seasons come and go, but Your love remains constant.
The tides rise and fall, but the tide of Your grace is
always high.
The economies of this world boom and bust, but Your
abundance always overflows.
Each moment our shadows shrink or grow, but in You
there is no shadow of change.
Before the oceans were hollowed out or the mountains
bulged up, from everlasting to everlasting,
You are God.
You are permanence personified.
In our world nothing lasts, nothing stays the same.
May Your eternal purpose give meaning to our
temporary pursuits.
In Your never-changing love may we find security for our
less-than-stable souls.
Thus may we trace our way through this transitory terrain
and join You at last in the unchangeable glory of Your
eternal kingdom.

Chapter 9

The Neighbor

Every morning this week at the Key Place I have awakened at first light to the familiar sound of a rooster crowing.

What's so extraordinary about that? you may ask.

The truly extraordinary aspect behind that quite common experience is my sudden awareness that never—not once in my seventy-plus years—have I greeted the dawn in this house without a rooster or two nearby to herald the occasion.

For purely practical reasons my industrious Key grandparents always had a patch full of chickens when I was a boy. Thanks to those busy birds, Grandmother Key sold eggs, scrambled eggs for our breakfast, supported African missions half a world away, and added to the cholesterol of dozens of gospel preachers who dined at her Sunday table. Every bit as much as cousins and puppy dogs, chickens were an accepted, unquestioned part of my world as I grew up. So in this house we were always awakened from our boyhood beds by the crowing of the cocks in the chicken patch out back.

But times changed as we grew older. As my grandparents' children migrated and the grandparents' finances improved, raising chickens made less sense economically. Why buy chicken feed, fix fences, gather eggs, chase foxes, kill snakes, and pluck feathers when eggs and fryers are so cheap and easy to get at the store just across the creek? So the day came when the chicken patch became just a patch. The chickens of our childhood became just a memory. And the weathered boards of the old chicken house, now cleansed of their distinctive odor by decades of rain and sun, came inside to serve as rustic wainscoting in the bathroom, a decade or so after the galvanized egg nests vanished to God only knows where.

All of our chickens were gone, but—and now I get to the point of this tale—the rooster's familiar matin was not muted at the Key Place. Still, in this old house, the sun is welcomed every dawn by the lusty call of the barnyard's sentinel. This morning was no exception. Through the open windows beside my bed I heard the rooster's first song and opened my eyes to see the first pink rays of the not-yet-risen sun tinting the deck of clouds that hovered on the eastern horizon.

As I lay there listening to the rooster's increasingly robust celebration, it dawned on me that I have our neighbor to thank for preserving this unchanging ritual of life at the Key Place. How many other places can you go in this modern world and hear a rooster greet each dawn?

Just across the road that borders our pecan orchard east of the house, this less-than-normal neighbor has lived as long as I can remember. She is a recluse—by now an aging one—who tends her goats and feeds her chickens and labors from dawn until dark every day to maintain and enlarge the shipping-pallet pens that house her noisy menagerie, whose company she seems to prefer to that of the humans who reside around her. But I quickly confess that this may be my subjective and possibly quite unfair perception. Maybe this lonely soul would give every shekel she possesses to have human companionship. God knows she has lived almost all her days without any.

By the time I was six or seven, I knew something was odd about this neighbor. In a time when all proper females wore lengthy locks and feminine dresses, this woman butched her hair, donned Levis, and did her best to look like a man. As kids in the 1940s, my cousins and my siblings and I were too naïve to discern anything sinister in this neighbor's choice of male attire, but even in that more innocent time, I'm sure the grown-ups harbored grave suspicions about what our neighbor was trying to tell us by the way she dressed. For all I know, this hardworking woman may simply have been dressing in the simplest and most appropriate costume for her reclusive lifestyle and animal husbandry activities. But folks in town didn't seem to perceive her in this light.

I don't recall any of our clan ever acting ugly or saying anything unkind to her, but I realize now that they did not seek her company—not like we did as we formed lifelong friendships with the churchgoing Smith family across the street. And, for the most part, this unusual neighbor kept to herself and tended to her own business, acting for all the world like she kind of preferred being left to herself. Increasingly, as the years have passed, she has isolated herself in her self-constructed agricultural alcove, without so much as a wave or a howdy to the rest of us who live adjacent to her secluded world.

Today it dawned on me for the first time that I owe this odd woman more than I know for preserving the aural flavor of my childhood all these years at the Key Place. Granddaddy's goats have been gone for decades now, but I doubt there has been a single day when we could not hear our neighbor's goats bleating right next door. And for three decades now, or four, this unusual neighbor has provided roosters to wake up the morn.

Transvestite is a word I had not heard when I first gawked at this mannish female creature in her masculine attire. But I did grow up knowing what God had to say about this sort of thing. I remember how uptight my parents were the first time my five-year-old sister wore a pair of girl's slacks on a visit to see the grandparents in West Texas. They fully expected each grandmother to express grave consternation at this imprudence, possibly bidding them to read again the stern warning of God's Word.

"The woman shall not wear that which pertaineth unto a man, neither shall a man put on a woman's garment," the trusty old King James Bible charges God's people, and then it explains, "for all that do so are abomination unto the LORD thy God" (Deut. 22:5). If my grandmothers had lived long enough to see the New International Version, I'm sure they would have welcomed its clarification of this divine command: "A woman must not wear men's clothing, nor a man wear women's clothing." Christians in their generation were serious about enforcing this law of God.

The clothing habits of our cross-dressing neighbor threw up a barrier that blunted the evangelistic zeal and neighborly instincts even in someone as loving and sweet and gentle as my dear Grandmother Key. Looking back, I now feel certain that Grandmother evaluated this woman's behavior through the strict scriptural interpretations common to that era. In her eyes, our neighbor was pushing God's envelope. She was seriously misguided. The only way Grandmother knew to be loving toward her was just to leave her alone.

So this separate existence—our neighbor in her world and us in ours—became the status quo. Of course, her goats and roosters don't know about social taboos like this. They don't know they're not supposed to talk to us. Thank God for the billy and the rooster, who, at least in this aspect, behave more wisely than we humans on both sides of this street corner.

"How do you know it's a rooster?" one of the more irreverent neighbors asked one day. In that barnyard, he suggested, maybe it's a hen!

People can be so terribly cruel—especially to those who are different than they are. I wonder if anybody in that small town—anybody who has seen or met this neighbor—has ever asked her point-blank why she dresses the way she does. For all these years has she really been making a statement about her sexual orientation, long before such statements were publicly acceptable? Was she two or three generations ahead of her time in that way, or could it be that she just preceded the sartorial tastes of Americans by a generation or two?

When I was a kid, women simply did not dress like men. By the standards of that day it was not acceptable. It cost our neighbor much scorn. Had she waited forty years to don pants and shear her locks, nobody in town would have noticed. Today she looks like half the females on Robert Lee's church pews. As one of my friends commented, if women wearing short hair and dressing in jeans and shirts means transvestism, every Wal-Mart in America is filled with deviant shoppers.

"Do not judge by appearances," Jesus cautions us (John 7:24 NRSV). Perhaps the righteous townfolks who shunned our neighbor on the basis of words in Deuteronomy needed to read the Gospels as well.

❧— ❧— ❧—

Some thirty years or so after this Key Place neighbor unknowingly introduced me to the topic of gender confusion, I got my first real insight into the huge amount of human hurt that lurks in this often-unseen segment of our world. That feisty little Irish nun, Sister Olivia Prendergast, whose retreat into silence I described to you earlier, enlisted my aid in hosting a clergy seminar at the local hospice where she was head of pastoral care.

In the years that followed, Olivia would become one of my dearest friends, but that year our friendship was just blossoming and she was chock-full of surprises fit to knock your socks off. The topic this demure nun chose for our clergy seminar that spring was homosexuality.

AIDS was just making its first headlines. People worldwide were terrified by what they were reading. Since at that moment our hospice was the only medical facility in the region that would offer care to people dying with AIDS, and since almost all of those patients were homosexuals, Olivia wisely felt that the leaders in all our area churches needed to get up to speed on the issues involved.

Thus began, for most of us who participated, a learning time that stretched our souls like none before or after it. We jumped—or perhaps I should say, Olivia pushed us—off the diving board into the deep end of a spiritual pool most of us had never swum in.

When Olivia taught us, she was not content for us just to read textbooks or listen to academic lectures by experts. We did some of that, to be sure, but Olivia felt strongly that we needed to be confronted with what she liked to call "living documents"—people who were struggling with whatever problem we happened to be studying at the time.

I will never forget the day during our homosexuality seminar when this little nun packed a small conference room with a dozen of us clergy types. Then she trotted out before us four living, breathing, somewhat anxious representatives of the local homosexual scene. For over two hours they talked to us nonstop.

To begin with, we heard from a dazzlingly attractive young black woman, who explained to us that she danced and sang in nightclubs all across the South and West. Our town was one of her smaller gigs, she said. Usually she was on stage in places like Houston or New Orleans or Atlanta. In a sultry, husky voice she shocked most of us when she told us how much she normally got paid by the clubs that employed her.

Imagine our consternation when, about half an hour into this rather tentative interview, this gorgeous performer revealed to us that she was a he. I don't think a single one of us had tumbled to the truth. This fake female had bamboozled us all. Once we knew the truth about this person, then our questions began to fly again—this time in earnest—as we "students" began to let the shocking reality of this encounter chip away at our naïveté.

We who usually labored inside churches were spending that afternoon with the top drag queen in the lower half of the United States, and the friends who had accompanied the performer to our seminar were all of them card-carrying members of the local homosexual community. How in the world did Sister Olivia unearth such a crew and gain their confidence sufficiently to convince them to take the huge risk of being vulnerable and candid with a gaggle of priests and preachers whom they normally would have avoided like the plague?

Years later Olivia told me that accepting her invitation and coming to the seminar that afternoon was their way of saying "Thank you" to her because she had shown unexpected grace and compassion to one of their buddies as he died a particularly traumatic AIDS death, and then, while family and former church friends stood aloof from them, she had seen the tears of the dead man's friends and offered comfort and care to them in their grief.

"By this shall all men know that you are my disciples: if you love one another," Jesus tells us. Sadly, the little cluster of homosexuals in our seminar room that day—and most of the people like them in our town—did not name "love" as the most common reaction of Christians to them and their kind. Like my neighbor at the Key Place—branded "transvestite" by so many of the proper folks around her—homosexuals seldom found any comfortable way to interact with the church crowd in town. The love Olivia had shown to them in the name of Jesus was so rare that they could only respond by agreeing to her request to come tell us their story face to face. But the story each of them related to us was harsh, angry, and in your face—full of hurt and fury that stemmed from years of treatment they perceived as rejection and condemnation.

One by one they told us how their early-life ties to family and classmates and church came unraveled when their sexual inclinations became known. Like most of their homosexual friends, these young adults felt unwelcome in their childhood homes, and none of them had any continuing relationship with a church. In response to our questions about this latter deficit in their lives, they poured out years of accumulated and often rehearsed rage, in some cases naming specific churches and pastors whose disapproval they had interpreted as hatefulness and censure. Nothing we pastors said to them in that brief face-off seemed to make the slightest dent in their unanimous perception that Christian churches had nothing to offer them except more condemnation and unacceptable pressure to reform their lives in matters they felt unwilling or unable to change.

As the afternoon wore on and our guests began to sense that we would not give angry answers to their hostility, they minced no words in telling us they perceived us and our churches as "the Enemy." Do I need to tell you that hearing this so bluntly put was terribly discomfiting to a band of veteran ministers who usually chose to see ourselves and our congregations as proclaimers of Good News and dispensers of grace? Our discomfort grew as we reminded each other that Jesus was always seen not as the judge but as the friend of sinners.

What had we and our fellow Christians in recent years done to forfeit that identity? Is there anything we can do to reclaim it? Short of condoning behavior the Bible clearly calls sin, what can the church of Jesus do to assure sinners that we offer them salvation instead of condemnation?

I find myself wondering: Does the owner of the rooster that waked me up in the Key Place this morning resent me and the other preachers and the churches in her town as much as that drag queen and her friends said they did? Is my neighbor's refusal to wave hello or to exchange a howdy the result of similar wrath bottled up in her soul, possibly accentuated by her feeling that most folks in town have falsely judged her? Has she been watching us come and go past her house and hating us all these years? And what about all the other people like her and like the drag queen and her cadre?

What could we followers of Jesus possibly do to be perceived as the friends of sinners?

Another rooster awakened the soul of another preacher long ago. Remember the bird whose second crow of the morning woke up Peter's conscience right after his shameful denial of his friendship with Jesus? The God who spoke to one errant preacher through the mouth of a donkey also seems to enjoy conveying his warnings through the cackles of witless fowls.

Peter got the Lord's point instantly. He turned and fled into the darkness, weeping for the wrong he had done.

I must confess that it took a lot of crowing for a lot of years before I heard the Lord's voice in that rooster's call. But You've got my attention now, Lord, and I'm listening.

Just a few months after I wrote this chapter about our alienated neighbor, she died. Well into her nineties, she had seemed like a permanent part of our neighborhood, almost as unchangeable as the land itself. Now, suddenly, she is gone. And, gone with her, are all her flocks and fowls. I was pleased to learn that the young Hispanic man who purchased her old house on that corner lot had been her close friend. She did not die friendless, as I had feared. He tells me that she begged him to move into her place after she had left it. In his months there he has sold or moved all the animals and hauled away all the aging, rotting pallet pens. When I ventured over to meet him, he was mowing the knee-deep weeds, trying to make the place look decent for the first time in decades. I told him how pleased I am to know that the lonesome former owner was loved by his family and how much I miss her rooster.

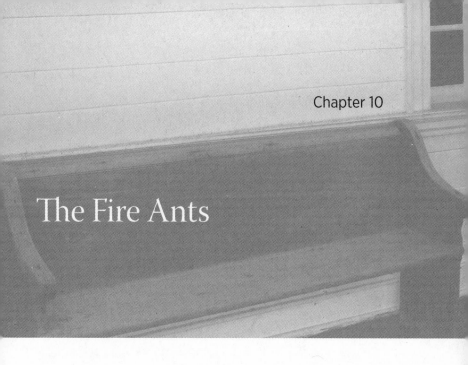

Chapter 10

The Fire Ants

When God told Adam that the earth which had nourished and delighted him in Eden was about to turn hostile to its keeper, he warned Adam about thorns and thistles, but he forgot to mention fire ants.

How appropriate that those vicious little beasts with a sting straight from hell should be one of the curses Satan turned loose on our world when he convinced us to reject the Creator's plan and do it our way.

Have you ever been stung by a fire ant?

I first saw these tiny demons at work in my parents' yard in Houston. "Watch out for the fire ants," my mother cautioned as I carelessly traipsed across the St. Augustine grass between the driveway and her front door. Without her warning I likely would have plodded squarely across one of the private sand piles the ants had so rudely deposited atop my parents' lush lawn. Anybody who has dealt with fire ants knows the result would have been instant disaster.

For years I fooled myself, falsely assuming that fire ants were just one of six dozen good reasons I can list for not living in Houston (sorry, Astro and Texan fans, for any slight to your concrete jungle). Fire ants are a southern phenomenon, I told myself. (So much so that the Yankee who put together the spell-check database for WordPerfect still thinks *fire ant* should be spelled as two words. Likewise all the dictionaries you can find, all of them unaware of the spelling we fire-ant exterminators read on ant poison labels. But we won't try to wage that battle here.) Lulled by my assumption that these voracious little devils were Gulf Coast pests that would not survive a good solid freeze up north, I was totally unprepared for their unwelcome invasion of the Key Place in the spring of 2003.

On every corner of the property that April I could see the tell-tale mounds that signaled the fire ants' arrival. On terrain where all of my days I have trudged with little or no vigilance, now I must measure every step with care. Woe to the mindless trespasser who dares to cross the chicken patch or the pecan orchard in the dark. If such an intruder's errant foot were to land on a fire ant mound, he'd soon be howling, dancing, shucking pants, slapping his extremities, and pleading for divine deliverance.

We all need some of that, of course. Divine deliverance, I mean. Ever since Satan slithered into Eden and beguiled our parents, the world we live in has been a mess and we humans have been locked in a death struggle with our mortality.

Do I need to tell you that the pain Satan dishes out to those who do his bidding makes the fury of angry fire ants seem tame in comparison? Some think our Lord's references to hellfire were metaphorical—spiritual images of curses beyond our most inflamed imaginations. Let me assure you that the fire Satan unleashes on sinners in this present world burns as hot as hell. No man or woman who has been through a divorce doubts this. Talk to any person whose lapse of honesty made the headlines and they will assure you that the fires of shame burned to the core of their soul.

In our fallen world, even totally innocent people tend to blame themselves endlessly for accidents that harm their loved ones. How much worse must be the guilt borne by those whose sins actually are to blame.

Genesis tells us that paradise was invaded. Ever since the Fall we sons and daughters of Adam have been falling. And, just like Adam and his wayward bride, we who bear their sin-laden DNA have been suffering the consequences of our wicked ways. America's great black poet, Dr. James Weldon Johnson, wrote one of his famous poetic sermons about the prodigal son.

> *Young man—*
> *Young man—*
> *Smooth and easy is the road*
> *That leads to hell and destruction.*
> *Down grade all the way,*
> *The further you travel, the faster you go.*
> *No need to trudge and sweat and toil,*
> *Just slip and slide and slip and slide*
> *Till you bang up against hell's iron gate*
> *(God's Trombones,* 22).

Some of us have "banged up against hell's iron gate," and it hurt. Bad. We have the knots on our heads and the scars on our souls to show for it. And it seems at times that some of the wounds simply won't heal. They last—long—like the poisoned welts left behind by fire ants.

Fire ants are on my mind because the last time I escaped to Robert Lee for a half-week-long reading and writing retreat, I foolishly forgot we had them. My brain was in neutral that week. The overload of incredibly onerous weeks just past evidently had taken their toll on my psyche. I was almost one hundred miles from home—over a third of the way there—when it dawned on me that I had driven off without loading my laptop computer. When I hauled my belongings into the Key Place in the semi-darkness of approaching night, I discovered that I also had failed to pack my work shoes, always a necessity for that prickly pear- and mesquite-infested terrain. Obviously I was mentally out of it that night.

In that state of semi-stupor, I hurried down to the water meter on the east perimeter of the property, eager to get the water running so the electric water heater could fill and I could switch on the power to the house before total darkness descended. It was already so dark that I grabbed a flashlight before I scurried out to turn on the water. I didn't want to play around inside that meter box before I checked to see if some freeloading scorpion or black widow had taken refuge there from the recent heavy rains.

All of my life—since my youngest days—I have known to be cautious in Coke County about such critters. Watching out for them is second nature when I'm at the Key Place. It is part of my DNA. But that night I forgot Coke County had ever seen a fire ant. That was a critical mistake.

Down on my knees, trying to protect my dress shoes and my Dockers from the moisture and mud of the previous day's rain, I quickly uprooted several handfuls of foot-tall ragweeds that were encroaching on the water meter box. With the flashlight and wrench in my left hand, I tried to lift the new meter box lid with my right one alone. It wouldn't budge. So I laid down the light and the wrench to free both hands for the task. Still the lid resisted for just a moment, causing my fingers to touch the surrounding soil ever so briefly as I wiggled the lid loose.

That's when I felt the first bite. Fire shot through my right hand. The flashlight was lying in the weeds, so it was too dark for me to see that some of the ragweed plants I just pulled had been rooted in a fire ant bed, and those horrid creatures from Dante's *Inferno* were not the least bit happy to be disturbed so unceremoniously at bedtime.

The ones I could see I slapped off both hands (actually succeeding in transferring mad ants from one hand to the other). By the time I got the water turned on and the meter box lid replaced, my hands and arms were covered with stings.

Fire ant stings become visible only the next day. And the next day. And for several days to come, in fact. The bite marks first surface on your skin as angry red spots, red sores with nerve endings aflame, with the poison then rising to a head in white pustules.

Each day after the attack for the rest of the week new red spots emerged on my arms and hands, giving new evidence of the original damage. The half dozen or so bites I thought I felt that night turned out to be at least two dozen or more. So it took a while for me to know how much damage the wicked little beasts had really done to me.

Is this further evidence of their satanic origin? Is this not precisely how Satan's damage emerges after we sin? The initial pain and panic of our guilt and shame assault our souls. But when they pass without immediate doom descending, we're not unlike Adam and Eve. "In the day you eat thereof, you will surely die," God told them about the forbidden fruit. But a day or so after their transgression they were still taking nourishment and kicking up dust. Death had not come. Not like they expected. After the initial shock, their fear of consequences temporarily abated.

Maybe things weren't going to be so bad after all.

Maybe the price of sin was not as high as the Creator had led them to believe.

Maybe Satan was right after all.

Then blow after unexpected blow—sting after unforeseen sting—the true injuries of their sin came to light, until finally, east of Eden, stripped of their real estate, ashamed of their very bodies, weary from suddenly fruitless labor, dreading the pains God promised, Adam and Eve hunkered down to endure the dying that did come upon them inexorably, and with pain made even less tolerable by the measured pace of its coming.

Sin often unmasks its dastardly damage like that, bit by agonizing bit revealing—sometimes long after the sin—just how grievously our misdeeds have wounded us.

Ask anyone whose extramarital affair is now cold enough for the customary hormonal blinders to be lifted, and they can catalog for you a sad list of ruined relationships, broken promises, damaged reputations, economic losses, legal confusions, and lost family moments that keep unraveling, seemingly without end. They will understand the parable of the fire ants with their time-release stings.

So will anyone who ever let a momentary loss of integrity tempt them to cover up their mistakes with a lie or to pad their budget with somebody else's dollars. How quickly the sin is done. How agonizingly slow but certain are the continuing revelations of bitter consequences set in motion by such misdeeds.

Like fire ant stings, the poison of sins committed often festers unseen until the evidence of our guilt bursts forth so raw and red and angry that everyone can see.

James said something like this: "Each one is tempted when, by his own evil desire, he is dragged away and enticed. Then, after desire has conceived, it gives birth to sin; and sin, when it is full-grown, gives birth to death" (James 1:14–15).

This tendency of sin with all its deadly potential to grow unobserved—off the scope—also caught the attention of the apostle Paul. "The sins of some men are obvious, reaching the place of judgment ahead of them; the sins of others trail behind them" (1 Tim. 5:24). "They show up later," *The Message* version tells us. Part of the deviousness of Satan is his ability to blind us to the extent of our wounds until we have hurt ourselves almost beyond repair.

With wisdom that must have come too late, some penitent soul remarked that "the trouble with most trouble is that it begins as fun." Moses recognized this. The Scriptures tell us that he was wise enough to know that "the pleasures of sin" are by nature temporary. Then, when the fun is over, comes the inevitable judgment.

By God.

By our associates.

And—perhaps worst of all—by our own consciences, as we rue our own pitiful failures and cry out with another famous sinner, "O wretched man that I am! Who will deliver me from this body of death?"

The morning after my encounter with the fire ants at the meter box, I arose from my bed with zeal to annihilate every last one of them that dared to move a grain of sand on our parcel of land. I drained the last yellow grain from our Amdro jug long before I had doctored even a third of the fire ant dunes on the Key Place. So I hurried down to cousin Joe David's feed store to replenish our stock of fire ant bait.

Do I need to tell you that it's not cheap? In my three-day campaign to rid my hunk of earth of this latest scourge, I think I spent more on food for the ants than for myself.

My fire ant stings eventually did heal. For weeks after my foolish encounter with those evil little beasts, though, I thought I had been permanently damaged by their venomous stings. The resulting sores just would not go away. But I remember looking down at my wounded hand one day a few months later and thinking, "The fire ant bites are gone. Without my even noticing it, the sores have vanished. That bad experience is over."

So it is with the guilt of our sins that "cling so tightly," to borrow the insightful description in the book of Hebrews. My friend Dr. Edward Fudge cites lines from an old hymn unfamiliar to me. I don't remember singing it, but I heartily subscribe to its truth:

Deep in the human heart, crushed by the tempter,
Feelings lie buried that grace can restore.

A more modern hymn also gets it right when it celebrates "grace that is greater than all our sins."

Regardless of how utterly we are crushed by our failures, regardless of how bitter may be the consequences of our sins, regardless of the depth of our remorse and embarrassment at having let down so many who loved and counted on us, still God's grace can heal our sinful hearts and Christ's blood can wash away the stains. And one day—after what seems like an eternity of grief and regret—we may be surprised to find ourselves whole and happy again in God's service. The stings of the fire ants are gone.

I think I am correct when I assume that I am describing here the experiences of all of us. "If any person says they do not sin," the apostle John bluntly insists that they are lying. *All of us sin.* And the more we hunger and thirst for righteousness, the more we agonize over the wounds caused by those sins. The more lasting is the sting of the fire ants of the soul. And the greater is our gratitude for heaven's grace.

My youngest son is a world-class scholar in the writings of the Christian poet John Donne. He alerted me to three lines by Donne that well sum up what I'm saying here. The poet prayed,

Look, Lord, and find both Adams met in me;
As the first Adam's sweat surrounds my face,
May the last Adam's blood my soul embrace.

What a shame that Christians through the centuries have turned Paul's great chapter 5 in Romans into a theological battleground. For in the last half of that chapter the apostle so clearly assures us that Christ undid all that Adam did to curse humanity. Through Adam came sin and death and eternal condemnation. Through Jesus came righteousness and life and grace for us all. In him alone can we find a cure for "the sting of sin."

Chapter 11

The Gates

We have multiple gates on the Key Place. At least, we have what is left of them. Most of them were huge, industrial-strength gates designed to control even the most rambunctious ranch animals. Then there were the two more delicate yard gates.

Granddaddy Key was an expert fence builder. Growing up in ranch country, he had worked with his father and his kin and his neighbors to build miles of fences back in the days when every fence post got cut from stands of cedar on their own place and every post required a hand-dug hole, often on rocky terrain. Tractor-powered augurs and jack-hammered T-posts were still several decades away. Fence-building in that part of West Texas back in the early 1900s was heavy, hard labor, but it was an art, and by the time our grandfather started to fence his adult home property, he was good at it.

None of us grandkids had even been thought of back in the days when Granddaddy constructed the Key Place stock pens, which basically were solid walls of seven-foot high cedar posts tightly strapped together with twisted coils of barbed wire. He

143

buried massive cedar corner posts four feet into the ground, leaving another seven or eight feet above ground to guarantee that those pens would hold just about any critter he needed to coop up. The gates on those sturdy pens were as rugged as the fences themselves—most of them pickup-wide, made of rough-hewn lumber bulkier than modern two-by-eights and swung on hinges so beefy no amount of weight would cause them to sag.

In their heyday those stock pens and gates appeared to be virtually indestructible. When we grandsons had to remove one of those corner posts and the gate hinged to it in order to dig a modern sewer line, we came away from that task declaring that those fences should easily stand until the end of time. But we were wrong. We failed to reckon on two inexorable forces: idleness and termites. Once the pens were no longer used every day to corral farm animals, they started wilting before our eyes. And the instant one of those monster gates began to drag on the red Coke County soil, it became termite bait. Only a few ragged remnants of the gates and random chunks of the antique hardware remain four decades after the pens were left idle and empty.

Curiously, the sturdiest fences died first. Just a few panels of those cedar-post fences still stand today, and they're threatening to lie down and quit any day now. But, at the same time, almost all of the more fragile wire-mesh fences our grandfather strung on solid cedar posts around the property's perimeter and around Grandmother's cherished yard are amazingly intact long after he died. Our grandfather built fences to last.

My brothers and I have been dribbling into Robert Lee this week, just as soon as each of us could wind up the tasks that tied us to our distant homes. More than once in the past three days I have chuckled to myself as I watched first one brother and then another on separate occasions pause to close and latch one of those smaller, more fragile yard gates. I caught myself doing it too. Gate-closing is one part of our raising that obviously stuck.

After supper this evening I sat out in the cool southeast breeze and studied the gate that separates the back yard from what used to be the chicken patch. What I saw intrigued me. As gifted as our grandfather was at building pens and gates to hold sheep or goats or calves or sows, he was obviously out of his niche when it came time for him to fashion the daintier, prettier gates he would install at the end of the sidewalks leading from the front and back doors of the house.

Always creative, he came up with a scheme to form rectangular gate frames using half-inch galvanized pipe with ninety-degree ells for the corners. With the kind of craftsmanship you would more likely expect from a quilting expert, somehow he managed to separate wires at the edges of the wire-mesh fences. Then deftly he wove and wrapped those extended edge wires around the pipe in a uniform, neat way that looked like something done by precision machinery in a factory. I can't imagine how he did it.

The pipes are beginning to rust a little now, and the wire is showing its age, but more than eighty years after they were conceived, the two yard gates at the Key Place are still incredibly intact. And they exert an almost magical power over my three brothers and me. We simply cannot walk through one of them without closing and latching it.

Gates. They're everywhere, aren't they? As I studied those ancient Key Place yard gates, I found myself reflecting on how much gates impact who we are and what we do every day.

Those of us who fly know about airport gates, don't we? Getting from one gate to the other can require quite a trek in a large airport like Chicago's O'Hare. Finding the right one is the only way to reach your intended destination.

All of my days in this part of the world I have heard people saying, "Well, it looks like he locked the gate after the cow was gone." I wonder: Is this a regional figure of speech heard only in farm and ranch country like Coke County?

When an unexpected flood of highway traffic blocks their path, West Texans also can be heard to grouse, "I wonder who left the gate open."

When Gateway Computers chose their name, I wonder if they realized how many layers of meaning lurked in that term. So much is said today about gateways to power, to knowledge, to services of all sorts.

With some slight indebtedness to John's metaphors in the book of Revelation, people talk about encountering St. Peter at the Pearly Gates. Regardless of who monitors that famous gate, most of us do hope to get through it, don't we?

When baseball announcers tell us how many fans paid for tickets to attend that night's game, we say that they are announcing "the gate."

We get into theme parks like Disney World and Sea World by going to their gates.

Some folks today are fortunate enough to live in what we call "gated" communities where burglars and Jehovah's Witnesses are less likely to come calling.

Racehorses ready to run the Derby are said to be "in the gate."

Of course, all of us have heard about Water*gate*. And far too many soundalikes after it.

If you grew up reading and hearing the King James Bible, as I did, you know the Matthew 16 promise that Christ will build his church on the Rock, "and the gates of hell will not prevail against it." Any preacher worth his salt can lambast a whole bevy of evils with a text like that—even if Jesus did mean something a bit different when he spoke those words originally.

Everywhere we go we keep bumping into gates, don't we? The first one I thought of when I let my mind shift from our assortment of Key Place gates was the gate Jesus referred to in his famous parable in John 10:7–9. Those of us reading these verses in the King James Version will not hear Jesus telling us, "I am the gate." Does using "door" (as the KJV and many other Bible versions do) instead of "gate" make it harder for us to catch the Master's drift?

His "gate" lesson in John 10 does seem to be a hard one for many in this present generation to stomach. Multiculturalists imbued with the postmodern gospel that all faiths are equally true (or false) tend to choke on Jesus' claim to be "the" entrance to God's blessings. "Whoever enters through me will be saved," Jesus promises, but many today are apt to reply that they can be saved just as surely by following Mohammed or Buddha or Moses. The Christ of the Gospels does not agree with this assertion, of course. He can be so offensively exclusive in his claims. Evidently it never occurs to him to try to be politically correct.

If the gate parable bothers somebody—with its mildly positive assertion that Jesus is *the* gate to salvation—how do you suppose they'll react when they hear Christ insisting four chapters later, "No one comes to the Father except through me"? Those are fighting words in an age drunk on diversity. Not only does Jesus claim to be the gate to God's favor; he baldly asserts that he is the only way to get there.

How can we convey this message to modern hearts without stirring up outrage instead of faith? Is it even possible, since so many today consider such a claim to be bigoted and gauche?

Will our natural desire to be liked and respected tempt us to soft-pedal our Lord's uncompromising claim? If we do, will he "show us the gate"?

Before my mind detoured into the contemplation of so many sorts of gates both physical and spiritual, I started to tell you how much it amused me this week to see what eerie control these aging Key Place yard gates exert on the behavior of my brothers and me.

Like puppets controlled by a master pulling our strings, we cannot walk through either gate—front or back—without pausing to close it and latch it by slipping the ancient rusty chain link over the equally rusty stud in the fence post beside it. We go through this ritual, almost without fail, even if we're going to be coming right back through the same gate just a few seconds later.

Why? Because many decades ago our grandparents and parents drummed it into our imprintable juvenile psyches that *the* cardinal sin of any child playing in the Key Place yard was leaving one of those gates open or unlatched.

The few times we did scamper off without securing one of the gates invariably proved the validity of the rule. In just a wink or two an open gate would let a dozen or more chickens invade Grandmother's carefully kept yard. To her horror she would find them in every flower bed, scratching and pecking at her tender bedding plants. Worse yet, those errant fowls could easily escape the whole domain by fluttering over the lower fence out front. Lost chickens were lost meals, lost eggs, lost dollars, when all of these were in short supply.

But any careless grandchild who mindlessly left the back gate unchained invited even greater catastrophe if Granddaddy's goats happened to be grazing in the chicken patch that day. With uncanny alertness for any open gate, it would take those voracious animals just an instant to begin dining on Grandmother's petunias or hungrily devouring the foliage on her pampered crepe myrtle or nandina bushes. The miscreant who left that gate ajar usually paid dearly for his sins. We learned that lesson almost before we were old enough to talk.

Today no chickens populate the patch outside the back fence. It has been at least three decades, nearer to four, since the last goat nibbled the weeds in areas surrounding the off-limits yard. So today the back gate protects the Key Place yard from absolutely nothing. And to render our present gate-closing behavior even more irrational, not more than thirty feet from the back gate two sections of the west fence are now missing—totally gone—mashed flat and demolished beyond repair by that tenant's hungry horse many years ago. So the entire yard is open and exposed to any inhabitants of the patch with or without that gate closed.

But still, just as we have done every time we have come in or out that gate for more than seven decades, B. and I compulsively shut and latch it. What is it the Good Book says about training up a child in the way he should go, and when he is old . . .?

Whether they are good or bad, habits are hard to break, aren't they?

Sharp parents make sure their kids learn good hygiene habits early. "With the Lava, Roger," the mother in that old TV ad insisted. Most moms are content if the hand washing gets done before their offspring plop down to dine. How blest is the person whose parents cared enough to teach them in their youngest days to brush teeth, comb hair, clean nails, and otherwise groom themselves. Such habits last a lifetime.

So do bad ones. Dirty words take root in our psyches like Johnson grass in a South Texas lawn. If you doubt that profanity is forever, just listen to the nursing home vocabulary of sweet little Christian ladies gone senile.

Addictions involve more than alcohol, tobacco, and drugs. Behaviors of all kinds ingrain themselves indelibly in our souls. Some people are like the woman in C. S. Lewis's delightful book, *The Great Divorce*. This gal bellyached and complained so much— she grumbled so often and so long—that Lewis says she just turned into a grumble. I've met a few of those.

Thankfully, I know some dear people who have developed the opposite disposition. They always see what's right about things. Some wise person a long time ago taught them to follow the apostle Paul's advice, "Whatever is true, whatever is noble, whatever is right, whatever is pure, whatever is lovely, whatever is admirable—if anything is excellent or praiseworthy—think about such things" (Phil. 4:8).

Many of our most valuable habits began as obedience to rules. I brush my teeth often because that was my mother's rule. She's dead now, but this rule-born habit still blesses me. Because our parents drilled that rule into us over and over again, most of us look both ways before we cross a busy street (and thereby stay alive). No doubt we could come up with a catalog of similar habits, many of them crucial to our continued health and survival.

But not all rule-based habits bless us. Some wag wanted to know why they sterilize needles for lethal injections. Why indeed? Rules that made sense in one time or situation may no longer apply. "Close the gates," made a lot of sense when our grandparents laid down that law. Today the reason for the rule has vanished and only the habit remains. I must confess that I am afflicted with a host of habits like that.

Even rules with divine origin, such as the dietary rules God gave the Jews, outlived their time and purpose. Jesus had the good sense to revoke them. Mark 7:19 tells us he "declared all foods 'clean.'" But a host of his followers in all the ages since then have insisted on binding those ancient Mosaic regulations on themselves and on their fellow believers.

Few of our habits are more deeply entrenched than our dietary preferences. The first President George Bush will never like broccoli, even if he lives to be a hundred. That's his prerogative, but it would be a foolish expression of self-denial if he avoided those healthy sprouts because of some out-of-date prohibition.

For his musical *South Pacific*, Oscar Hammerstein wrote the lyrics for his memorable song, "You've Got to Be Carefully Taught," with its obvious truth that no one is born with racial hate. We have to be taught. Wahhabi Muslims have to teach their little kids to loathe Americans, just as white Baptists in Mississippi in 1930 had to teach their children to fear and shun the black residents who lived just outside their town. The habits of our hearts and minds, as well as those of our hands, are learned responses, and we find to our distress that they are incredibly hard to unlearn.

Our mother's stern admonitions to "come back and latch that gate" still ring in my ears and control my bodily motions decades after her departure from this earth. Would that I remembered and still obeyed the useful lessons she taught me as well as I comply with her now meaningless instructions about closing those gates.

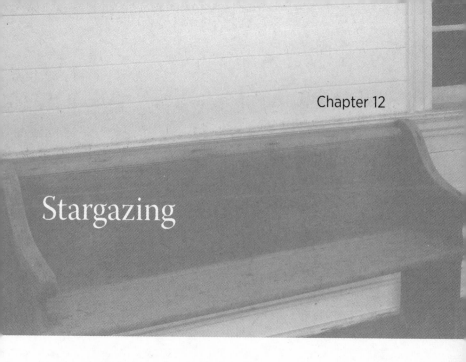

Chapter 12

Stargazing

Do you like stars as much as I do?

Stars have always fascinated me, ever since my mother's father took time to help us preschool grandkids locate the Dippers—both Big and Little—and the North Star, of course. Also Orion with his star-studded celestial belt, and the planets that show up early each summer night as the sun's glow fades in the western sky.

One evening last June I sat in the back yard of the Key Place—my favorite stargazing spot in all the world—and I watched the moon come up over the pecan orchard.

Just one night shy of full, that bright moon lit up a silver crest atop a bank of storm clouds south and east—clouds close enough to tantalize us in that parched land, but too far away to cool the summer night.

As I watched the moon inching ever nearer to the top rim of the thunderheads, suddenly in the sky high above them I spotted that evening's first star. At least it looked like a star. That laser-tip of light so intensely bright shone high in the southeast sky. "Something's wrong here," I thought. "That's not where the first star of the night is supposed to appear."

After a moment's reflection I decided that I probably was ogling some man-made hunk of space junk, far enough up there to catch rays of the sun which had just slid below the western horizon. From where I sat, though, it looked not at all like garbage but more like some celestial body effulgent with glory. Since we don't have anything else to worry about these days, scientists warn us that at least nine thousand pieces of abandoned hardware are now floating above us in space, some of them weighing tons, and all of them waiting for the right moment to plummet earthward.

Having been fooled by that hypocrite star, I now began a serious search for the real McCoys, Venus and Mars. I peered into the western sky, but it was still too light for me to see them. Since my main purpose that night was to do absolutely nothing, I loitered beside our huge Arizona cypress west of the house and waited for those tardy planets to pop out of the dusk.

Then for some reason it dawned on me that I was lounging right where Granddaddy Key first introduced me to the mystery of the stars sparkling in the night. How fitting, it seemed to me, that I should keep returning to that same spot to gaze again into the blackness of the heavens in search of its light. No wonder I still treasure this spot as one of the key places in my world.

Right in that exact place over seventy years ago, I also recalled, Grandmother Key first taught me the childhood jingle:

Star light, star bright,
First star I've seen tonight.
I wish I may, I wish I might
Have this wish I wish tonight.

Oh—let me tell you—on those summer nights so long ago, lying on my back in the Bermuda grass in Grandmother's yard, I wished some glorious wishes. And, with the sort of faith that is possible only to a four-year-old, I fully expected those wishes to come true.

Is Jesus thinking about something like this when he tells us we have to become like children to make it into God's kingdom? Unless we are humble like they are, he says, unless we have simple faith like they do, we'll never catch on to what God is up to in our world.

From childish wishes on a star we graduate as adults to fervent prayers to the God who loves us. But the active ingredient in both cases is unlimited faith.

I'm not sure I have that. Ask me if I believe the promises of God and I will assure you that I do. But then I read in the Gospels the strange story about the blind fellow who asked Jesus to fix his defective eyes, and Jesus responded to his request by telling him, "May it be to you according to your faith." In other words, "I'll make you able to see as much as you think I can." And this story shakes my soul, because it makes me wonder how much *I* would have been able to see if I had been that man. It makes me wonder even more if Jesus imposes that same limit on what he can and will do for me today.

Jesus is right, of course. Little children have the gift of unlimited faith. I hope Madeleine L'Engle is right when she posits in her book *Penguins and Golden Calves* that "our capacity for belief is greatest when we are children *and when we are old*" (135).

Those are my italics. If those words are true, maybe I'm on the brink of a time when my own feeble faith will deepen and, like the child who wished years ago on a star, I will begin again to fully expect God to hear and answer my prayers.

That modern apostle to persecuted Jewish Christians, Richard Wurmbrand, shares a curious reflection along this line. Somewhere in his book, *Christ on the Jewish Road*, he comments that along the way our sophistication and education may actually be handicaps. "Intellectuals," he says, "are seldom capable of conveying a message just as they have received it, without giving it a personal twist; whereas the simple, ignorant people transmit it faithfully" (159).

Not only must we become childlike to pray effectively, then, but if Wurmbrand is right, we may need the same simple childlikeness to faithfully communicate for the Lord—to keep from putting our spin on his gospel.

Whenever I retreat to the Key Place, usually hoping primarily to restore some semblance of peace and sanity to my frenetic soul, I find that few things help me more than pausing at sundown to welcome that evening's stars. I did it again tonight (more than a year after the moments described above). I watched the stars pop into place one by one in the darkening western sky.

This is good star-watching country. What clouds we get don't tend to last very long in this near-desert territory. And it's still dark enough here to actually see the stars. Rural sites are always best, of course—far away from any big city's luminescent haze—but small towns will work. They beat big ones every time for gazing at nighttime skies. So I take advantage of the rural darkness whenever I come to this sparsely settled place.

Maybe I was impatient, but the stars seemed to be shy tonight. They took longer to appear than I expected. April has just begun when I write these words. Maybe the planets tonight were like some of my church folks who forgot to set their clocks for Daylight Saving Time last Sunday and showed up late for worship.

Venus finally did show her face. I had been looking for her in the wrong place. She had strayed south, nearer to the western horizon than I anticipated. By July she'll be back where she "belongs." I'm a summertime stargazer, you see. Always have been. Spring and winter orbits seem wrong to me. The stars have got it right, of course, and as usual I'm the one out of sync with the universe.

Orion finally shuffled onto the celestial stage tonight. Then, as if reassured by his bravado, all around him pinpoints of light began to peek out of the deepening darkness.

Did you see where some modern Magi—astronomers in some big-name university's stargazing program—made headlines by announcing to us commoners that the constellation we call Orion is actually a cauldron of activity, with chunks of heavenly matter hurtling constantly through the massive spaces between the stars we earthlings see?

Somehow that revelation played hob with my lifelong admiration of the old warrior. I wonder sometimes if we can get too smart, learn too much for our own good. Part of the grandeur of heaven surely awes our souls precisely because there is so much we don't know about it. If it were possible to scientifically chart and quantify and factually analyze the eternal realms of glory, surely we earthlings would be the losers for it.

Majesty and mystery owe so much to each other. The Almighty God who won't let his creatures look at his face surely knows this.

If a decade from now NASA's Pluto probe returns to Earth with core samples from that distant world, and if I'm still around to hear the news, I'll be just as excited as the next guy. But I suspect that the knowledge we thereby gain of the edges of our visible universe will shrink it for us one more time, and we will be robbed of another layer of celestial mystery.

But I digress. I was telling you about my evening of stargazing here at the Key Place.

A strange thing happened to me tonight while I was waiting for the early stars to emerge in the sky. The dying glow of the sun still backlit the western horizon with a faint tint of orangish pink when I was startled by my own shadow, cast not by the vanishing sun—now much too faint for that—but by the bright half moon almost directly overhead.

Moon shadows always surprise me.

The dark spot on the ground moved quickly—when I did—and made me flinch. Had some nocturnal varmint grown weary of waiting for the recalcitrant stars and ventured up from the creek bed to prowl before his appointed hour?

I had to chuckle. The only varmint anywhere near was me.

By now the stars were multiplying rapidly. Earlier they had seemed timid, slow to expose themselves to this heavenly voyeur. I had counted the first tiny orbs one by one as they popped into place. When I got through being freaked out by my own nocturnal shadow, I turned my eyes heavenward once more to watch the sky overflow with countless points of light. And as I watched the Creator's nightly extravaganza, I recalled Isaiah's faith-filled lyrics.

"Lift your eyes and look to the heavens," the old prophet asked his people. *"Who created all these?"* And then he answered, *"He who brings out the starry host one by one, and calls them each by name. Because of his great power and mighty strength, not one of them is missing"* (40:26).

Isaiah was my kind of guy. He gazed at the stars and saw the face of God.

How, I wonder at times, could any thoughtful person contemplate our solar system and the uncountable galaxies beyond it without being moved to marvel at the mind and might of the One who first dreamed it and made it?

Even the pagans in ancient times and distant lands—people who had never read Judeo-Christian Scriptures or heard the name of Jesus—were moved to worship when they studied the stars. From Egyptian pyramids to Stonehenge pillars to Inca temples we find evidence that in all ages and cultures people who have pondered the planets have been driven to prayer. As Christians we may not agree with their myths or pay homage to the cruel gods and goddesses they created, but we do acknowledge the wisdom and share the instinct that drove these people to faith and humility when they looked up and saw the stars.

But it is not so for those who recognize no intelligence greater than their own theories, who acknowledge no power that transcends the technologies of their own age, who bow down to no god besides the puny ideals they have dreamed up and set in place. People with no faith look at the stars and see only cold, empty, fathomless space. For them the face of God is invisible. And many of them don't want anybody else to see him there either.

Recent challenges to the teaching of intelligent design in America's schools are but a rehash of the denials of skeptics who for at least four centuries have been trying to cast God out of the academy and out of the lives of all thinking citizens.

In early Renaissance days, Thomist scholars attempted to debunk medieval superstitions by training educators to deny God any legitimate role in social, scientific, or philosophical studies. This led to the barren years of Marx and his ilk, when the Russians mothballed their churches and jettisoned God from all political, economic, or medical instruction, while at the same time Darwin's godless theories of our origin were surfacing in the United States.

Then came the heady days in the 1970s when American educators proudly proclaimed that "God is dead" and done with for good. And now, since God refused to believe his obituary and vanish accordingly, judges on both coasts of the United States have taken up the cause, telling us it is illegal in America's public schools to give God any credit for creating his world.

In Psalm 8, David tells us he looked at the heavens and saw the works of God's fingers; he studied the sun and the moon that God had set in place, and it made him marvel at how insignificant humans must be compared to a Creator who could fashion the beauty and intricacy of such a universe. But today a brilliant agnostic studies the same stars and comes away without seeing the slightest hint that our God—or any god—exists. Having reduced reality to nature only, the unbelieving philosopher or scientist observes the vastness of the heavens and still sees nature only. Thus impoverished by their self-limiting definitions of life, they blind themselves to the God who reveals himself to the rest of us as we gaze at his stars.

Sometimes, living as I do most of the time in a city whose lights hide the glories of the night sky, I get to feeling as if I'm way behind on my stargazing. Not the astrology kind. I'm not into that hocus-pocus. But I get downright hungry to get back to that backyard perch on the west side of the Key Place, to reclaim my ringside seat to God's nightly light show.

Have I told you already? Stargazing isn't as good here as it used to be. In the past two or three decades my neighbors in Robert Lee have gotten all sissified and citified. They want paved streets. (I'm all for that.) But they also want streetlights. Bright mercury vapor streetlights. Lights that pollute the night sky and haze over the once-brilliant stars. I'm sure they won't agree with me, but, being a lifelong star-watcher, I feel that lighting up every corner of this quiet little town to keep from being robbed has, in fact, robbed us of far more than we have gained.

But I just now started to confess to you that in recent times I have not spent nearly enough time pondering God's planets. And that deficit is not entirely because I haven't tried.

On five evenings out of a single month last spring I settled into an easy chair in my stargazing spot here at the Key Place, eager to watch God trot out his brightest hosts for their nightly grand entry. I'm always ready to do that if the weather is even halfway cooperative, but I had added motivation to spend those nights watching the stars.

During most of April and May that year—so we were advised by folks supposedly in the know about such things—five of Earth's sister planets would align themselves diagonally right above the western horizon at sunset. This stellar performance would not happen again until I'm 103, we were told, so I wanted to see it this time. I'm not sure my eyes will be working all that well next time around.

"*The heavens declare the glory of God,*" one psalmist sang. "*Night after night they display knowledge*" (19:1–2). Not many pages ago we heard Isaiah's amazement at the fact that one by one God "*calls forth his hosts by name,*" and "*not one of them is missing*" (40:26). So I realize I'm not the only believer who has been fascinated by the stars.

But I was disappointed. If those five planets appeared on cue, I missed their performance. On each of my five stargazing nights, thick clouds shrouded the western sky. My best efforts to see this astral phenomenon were thwarted. And that frustrated me. When

I come to the Key Place and don't get to see the stars, I leave feeling cheated.

Do you suppose God was giving me a lesson in faith when he clouded over that planetary marvel? "We walk by faith, not by sight," the Scriptures tell us. I didn't have to see those planets to believe they were in their appointed places. Just like I don't have to see God to know he's there for me. All the time.

Chapter 13

The Bells

I have been lounging for the past couple of hours in the living room of the Key Place on the old couch my youngest brother Jim made with his own hands. I've been reading Philip Yancey's book *What's So Amazing About Grace?* while soaking up a deliciously cool breeze that has wafted from the southeast through the open front door and out the bevy of windows on the living room's west wall.

As I sat there reading, for some reason (could it have been the prompting of God's Spirit?) I began to think about a fellow I have known all of my life in this small town.

Since the man I'm thinking about is still alive when I am writing these words, I won't use his real name, but Rolf Jones will duck his head and honestly admit, if you ask him, that he hasn't darkened the door of the church in years.

He knows better. His saintly mama raised him to do better. When Rolf and his brother were growing up there in my mother's hometown, their family was in church every time the saints assembled and lots of times in between. I remember times when all of us got together to sing the songs of the church, the way we used to before Little League and TV took over the hours church folks once devoted to Stamps Baxter and Fanny Crosby and Beethoven.

I don't know what caused Rolf to turn his back on the church. Some of the squabbling that went on between church leaders when he and I were boys would have been enough to turn off any thoughtful soul. In that tiny town the church split. One bunch of Christians locked the other bunch out of the little church building one Lord's day, all because they couldn't agree on whether it was right or wrong to tell Bible stories to their kids before church on Sunday morning. Brothers and sisters who had loved each other dearly set up camp four blocks apart and spent the next several decades learning to disdain each other in the name of the Lord. All of this might explain Rolf's total lack of interest in church today. That whole mess certainly does disgust me.

Maybe he had personal problems I don't know about. Rolf has always seemed like a decent guy to me. I've never known him to be anything but honest and friendly—neighborly in the West Texas sense of the word. But you never know what might be going on in a fellow's heart and mind. Rolf strikes me as a guy who has too much integrity to sit on a church pew and pretend to be Mr. Clean when something's going haywire in his life. Like some other fine people I know, Rolf may be too good a man to go to church in the shape he's in.

Right now I suppose that only God and Rolf know why Rolf has dropped out of church and walked away from the faith of his childhood. And only God may know what it will take to bring him back.

But as I hung out in my grandparents' old house this morning, reading and meditating to refill my almost empty spiritual well, I had a strange inkling that God may now have his outreach to

Rolf in place. I think it's entirely possible that God may get to Rolf again by the bells.

Have I told you about the bells? They ring every hour. Atop the Methodist church. No bigger than Robert Lee is, I think you can hear them all over town. Especially if the wind happens to be blowing your direction, as it has been for me all morning. I know you could hear them today at Rolf's house.

Have the Methodists' bells been in disrepair and silent for some years? Or could it be that they were installed in the months since my visit to Robert Lee last fall? I don't recall hearing them before. They don't just chime the hour like Big Ben. Every hour they play a hymn. The very hymns Rolf and I and our families used to sing together. Hymns that speak of God's love and mercy and grace. Hymns that call us to love and follow Jesus.

As the bells chime the familiar melodies, my mind automatically supplies the words. I bet Rolf's does, too.

> *Fairest Lord Jesus, Ruler of all nature,*
> *O Thou of God and man the Son.*
> > *Thee will I cherish,*
> > *Thee will I honor,*
> *Thou, my soul's glory, joy, and crown.*

Really, Rolf? Is he really your soul's joy? As you sing it in your head, does it say anything to your heart?

At 2 p.m. the bells chimed,

> *Come, Thou Almighty King,*
> *Help us Thy name to sing.*
> *Help us to praise.*
> > *Father all glorious,*
> > *O'er all victorious,*

Come and reign over us, Ancient of Days.

Did you hear it, Rolf? As you sang along silently with the chimes, did you mean it?

Those Methodist bells have got to be working on Rolf's heart. A fellow can't engrave those hymns on his heart when he's a boy and then turn them off when he's a man. Visit any nursing home sing-along and you'll see that the music of faith stays intact in our hearts and minds when everything else departs.

Faith of our fathers, holy faith, the bells rang an hour later. *We will be true to thee 'til death.* I hope Rolf was listening, and maybe humming along.

Did he unconsciously sing with the bells,

What a friend we have in Jesus,
All our sins and griefs to bear?

I hope so. Whatever it was that came between Rolf and the church of our youth, what he needs right now is Jesus.

I have spent most of this day listening to the bells, and praying that Rolf was listening, too.

Wouldn't that be just like God? What a grand heavenly joke it would be if the Lord used those Methodist bells to beckon a straying non-instrument Campbellite back toward home.

Thinking so much about Rolf today got me to pondering a broader question. How do you speak about Jesus to your neighbor who won't discuss the subject with you?

Oh, your unchurched neighbor will talk to you about some things. About the Cowboys, and the weather, and the nutty federal policies that get his dander up. But he turns you off in the flick of an eyelash if you even mention church or Scripture or Jesus.

Perhaps something happened years ago to make this decent fellow allergic to religion. No telling now just what it was, because he won't talk enough about it to give you even a hint.

Maybe his father was one of those nuts who talk about Jesus all day and act like the devil all night. More than one person I know is running from the Father above because of the wounds they suffered from their father here on earth.

Could it be that your neighbor grew up in a church that substituted their traditions and legalisms for the loving commandments of the Almighty, and the guy was too smart to fall for that kind of a shell game? Like some good men and women all of us know, maybe your neighbor rejects anything remotely connected to Christianity because he doesn't know that he's never seen the real thing. Maybe that's why he doesn't want to hear about your faith.

One of the most decent guys I know stayed away from church religiously for over two decades because he couldn't stomach the hatefulness he kept hearing there. Surely, he thought, it can't be Christian to hate your fellowman in the name of Jesus. But that's what he heard from the pulpit and around the potluck table when he went to church with his wife on Sunday—vicious hatred aimed at blacks and homosexuals and Catholics and women who don't know their place.

In fact, the preaching my friend heard from these folks who claimed to be the only right and righteous believers in the county strongly implied that anybody who differed with them even a hair's breadth was a sinner headed straight for the fires of hell. That included him, he supposed, because he didn't agree with a lot of what they said. So finally he told his wife that he'd just stay away.

Maybe your neighbor who's turned off by church had a similar experience. It could be that he just has too much sense to buy into hatefulness like that.

Christian journalist Philip Yancey says he was like that. "I rejected the church for a time because I found so little grace there," he writes. After some years away, he did come back to the faith. "I returned," he says, "because I found grace nowhere else."

Of course, you and I really don't have a clue at this point as to why your neighbor (or your cousin, or your best buddy at work) is so touchy about religion. All we know for sure is that you've got a problem. You want to tell this person about the grace of the Lord, and he refuses to listen.

That's the problem I began to ponder when Rolf and the bells intruded on my reverie. *How do you talk to somebody about Jesus when they have made up their mind not to hear you?*

It's not just your hypothetical neighbor who doesn't want to hear the gospel. Virtually every non-Christian in our culture who has passed their tender childhood years has already decided that church and Bible and preaching and worship are not for them.

Recent studies show that ninety percent of all conversions to Christ happen before the age of fourteen. Beyond that point the door to our hearts gets so much harder to open. "Behold, I stand at the door and knock," Jesus says. But a host of our relatives and neighbors have barred the door and locked it tight, and they do not intend to answer.

In the Gospels Jesus says, "Those are the folks I'm after."

"I came not to call the righteous, but sinners, to repentance," he explains.

When straight folks criticized him for spending too much time with the derelicts and the high rollers of his day, he told them, "The Son of man came to seek and to save the lost."

The stories our Lord told made this point clearly. A shepherd who misses one of his lambs spends far more energy and time searching for the one he's lost than he does fussing over the ones who are okay. When he finds that sheep that strayed, he's jubilant.

That's our Lord. He loves us. All of us. But his burning concern is for the lost.

Can you imagine God as a housewife giggling and whooping with joy, dancing a jig around the den and down the hallway because she's just found the priceless heirloom coin that she thought was lost forever? That's how Jesus pictured God. He says that's the attitude of heaven toward the lost.

Three parables Jesus told there in what we call Luke 15—parables about a lost sheep, a lost coin, and a lost son. Because of the King James vocabulary, we call him the "prodigal" son.

Can you imagine how receptive the prodigal was to news from Daddy and the farm back home while he was bellied up to the bar with his newfound friends? He wouldn't have given you the time of day if he thought you wanted to remind him of his shirked responsibilities back home. But the father's heart followed that boy. His loving, grieving eyes looked down that road day after day, hoping, praying, longing for the son who had gone away.

The stories Jesus told describe his own heart, his own passion for those who are lost. And those lost ones are usually the hard ones to reach. Like my neighbor Rolf, they don't intend to be found, so they make it tough. *If we are going to be like Jesus, the deepest passion of our faith will be for those lost souls.*

Sometimes I think evangelism is like harvesting the pecans here at the Key Place. Some souls are like the pecans clustered on the lower branches of the tree. You can just reach right up and pluck them by the handful. They're easy to gather. But some of the finest pecans cling almost out of reach on the highest branches, and they're hard to get. A few times I've left the orchard crestfallen because I was unable to dislodge that last, distant, stubborn nut.

Those top pecans, the tough ones, are the ones I'm talking about right now. How do we reach those who seem determined not to be reached by the Lord?

Reaching people who are thoroughly lost is never easy, so I can't give you any neat formulas or quick, easy answers for touching their hearts. I suppose there are as many different ways to evangelize as there are people who need to be evangelized. It well may be that if you and I can't get the conversation started, God can.

How will God talk to your neighbor who won't talk to you about God?

I don't know. But I'm convinced that the God who hunts until he finds his lost sheep, the God who turns a house upside down to locate a lost coin, the God who never stops yearning for his straying child will never quit trying to reclaim his own.

To his love, add your daily prayers, and see what God can do.

The same bells that set me to thinking that morning about Rolf and wandering souls like him got me in trouble a few years later.

I had been back to Robert Lee for several days, once more intent on using this special place to replenish my spiritual juices. It was a warmer than usual spring week, with daytime temps too high for me to comfortably read or write inside the house during the hottest afternoon hours, so out in the yard I spied out any shady spot that was exposed to the infrequent wisps of wind, and I perched there while I read snatches of Madeleine L'Engle's *Two-Part Invention*, in which she journals the final, arduous weeks of her husband's dying.

I was out there trying to hide from the intense rays of the afternoon sun in the thinning shade of our dying Arizona cypress tree, when I again became more than normally conscious of the church bells. That night after the setting of the sun drove me inside to work under the light above the old kitchen table, I wrote this column which ran a few weeks later in my church newsletter and in newspapers all across the Texas Panhandle:

I am caught up in a war today—an unwilling participant—victimized by what I must conclude is either the ignorance or the callousness of a neighbor.

I come here to this small town to find a slower pace and a quieter space, a place to read and write. And place to think and just to *be*.

Today, however, is anything but quiet.

Three blocks east toward town a Hispanic family recently has moved into an aging hovel. Inside the house someone (a teenaged son, perhaps?) has a sound system that must fill his bedroom.

In the normally quiet mid-afternoon hours I like to read in the shade of the Arizona cypress in my west yard. But today this is not fun. The throbbing, pulsating boom of bass notes rapes the afternoon stillness. The raucous music invades all ears for blocks around.

When they first installed mercury vapor streetlights in this tiny rural town, I groused about the light pollution. Now I am even more distressed by the advent of all-day noise.

At the stroke of 3 P.M., however, my ear detects competition. In the tower of the brown-brick Methodist church only a few doors from the source of the afternoon's racket, the bell strikes the hour. And then I hear those chimes, louder still than the offending boom box, playing the hymn of the hour, "Lead, Kindly Light."

Yes, my heart responds. That's a sound and a prayer I can embrace. Then I find myself wondering. Does the teenager who owns those monstrous sub-woofers feel as violated by the hymn as I do by the pounding beat of his unsolicited concert?

Here I am, unwittingly caught in what feels like a cultural battle zone, where ancient hymns compete with modern ethnic ballads.

Is this also a battle of faith? I know the words to the hymn. At this distance, I hear only the wail but not the words of the Mexican music. So I can't be sure. Are the teenager's songs unchristian? Like so many modern songs, do they celebrate sin?

"Crown Him with Many Crowns" the chimes rang out an hour later. At 5 P.M. the hymn is "Abide with Me." By now the teenager has turned off his music. At least for now the Methodist carillon has outlasted him.

But, before I can celebrate the victory, reality whispers in my ear that the young musician will likely outlive both the aging bell tower and me.

As I massaged this column, honing its wording and trying to convey to my readers the complex welter of emotions triggered in my heart by that afternoon's experience, I stopped and pondered the adjective *Hispanic*. Would it cause some reader to think I was launching a racist tirade against my neighbors with brown skin? That certainly was not a message I intended or one I wanted to send.

At one point I actually deleted the word to see if the column still "worked" without it. And I tinkered with my wording in several other places, trying to remove any hint that my umbrage that afternoon was focused on the teenager instead of his choice of music and the mind-numbing volume thereof.

In the final newspaper version of the column, *Hispanic* had found its way back into the text. I could not think of any other way to characterize the cultural dissonance between the two kinds of music than to include the true fact that the town that afternoon was subjected to competing waves of Methodist and Mexican music.

My concerns that I might draw accusations of being racist turned out to be right on target. The column ran in the Hereford *Brand*, in a community that has a significant percentage of Latino residents. One woman got just as far as the word *Hispanic* and went ballistic. She sat down and wrote me a scathing letter, confessing my sins and disavowing any sympathy for any form of Christianity that I might be remotely connected to.

When I first read this angry woman's indictment, I was aghast. She had never met me. She had never heard me preach. She knew nothing about my long, close, mutually respectful ties to many Latino friends. That single ethnic identifier in my column convinced her that everything I wrote beyond that point was a virulent racist attack on all people of Spanish descent. In my thirteen years of newspaper column writing up to that moment, this was the most vicious response any reader had offered to anything I wrote—and there have been some real lulus. It goes with the territory.

After I read this woman's letter, I immediately emailed one of the editors at the *Brand* and requested that they print it if the woman had sent a copy to them as well. Nothing blesses a column, builds readership, and evokes support for a columnist more than a gratuitous, over-the-top attack like the salvo this woman had leveled at me.

Good sense would have told me to file that abusive letter without bothering to reply. It was apparent that the woman's mind was made up without any evidence on which to base her harsh conclusions, so I had to know that nothing I might say to her was likely to penetrate her judgmental spirit.

Again I was right on target. But I always have made it a practice to offer a personal reply to any identifiable person who takes time to respond to something I write. If somebody cares enough to write, they deserve to hear back from me. So I wrote her and tried to answer some of her more serious charges.

The letter I got back from her made the first one sound like a love letter. I filed the second ugly letter without reply, remembering our Lord's warning about casting one's pearls before those who by nature will respond by ripping you up. That was not the best month of my life.

This week—many months after the boom-box column tiff—I am back again at the Key Place. I'm pleased to report that the owner of the boom box has grown up and moved to the big city, taking his noise-producing equipment with him. I am even more delighted to note that, at least when the windows are open and the wind wafts from the southeast, here in my grandparents' old house you can still hear the church bells clearly, every hour on the hour, playing the great hymns of our faith.

But I realize now that the message of the bells is a mixed message, at least when that message is transmitted and translated through my inept words. While I hope it has penetrated Rolf's heart with a reminder of God's grace in Jesus, it also has enraged my Hereford reader, whose soul is just as precious in God's sight.

No single message or strategy of evangelism will reach every heart. We still draw people to Jesus one lost soul at a time, and only in his good time.

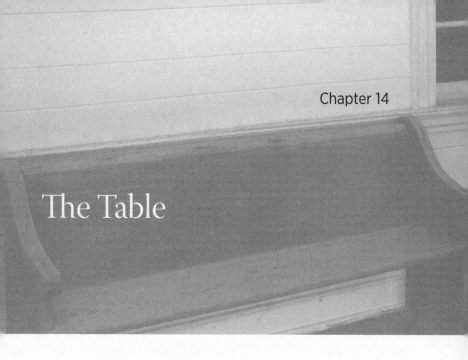

Chapter 14

The Table

Over seventy-five years ago I sat at this table for the first time. I was in a highchair, and my mother's parents were making over me as foolishly then as I dote on my own grandkids today. Of course, I don't remember much about that occasion, but it is truly the beginning of this tale, which is replete with memories that are vivid and poignant as they surface anew so many years after the events they archive.

In many ways the story of this old table is my story. Let me describe it to you.

Nothing about it is elegant. This table was built to last. With heavy five-by-five legs and with rails made of two-by-sixes in the old-fashioned lumber dimensions of the 1920s, it is as sturdy as the oak tree it came from over eighty years ago.

This piece of furniture was made to use, not to admire. Nobody went to the trouble to sculpt any part of it with a lathe or to rout decorative patterns on any edge. Sometime—perhaps in the late '50s—my grandfather refurbished it. He added the umpteenth coat of milk chocolate brown paint (did paint back then come in any other color?), and he covered the worn top with rugged marble-gray linoleum expertly fastened down by the sturdy stainless steel kitchen cabinet edging common to that era. He chose that material wisely. After more than sixty years of heavy use and equally severe neglect, the top is still flawless.

This table stands solid, like Gibraltar, without a creak or wobble in its frame. It is the Humvee of tables.

Four generations of my family have eaten meals, played games, scribbled Sears and Roebuck catalog orders, snapped beans, churned butter, bottled milk, folded clothes, cooled cookies, shared coffee, written sermons, bathed babies, sorted eggs, read the *Saturday Evening Post*, consumed homegrown fried chicken, sent email, and studied the Bible at this table. In a small house with precious little room for other pieces of furniture, this table is the place where we did virtually anything that had to be done in my grandparents' home.

Although the table fills the kitchen it stands in, it never seemed to be big enough. Back when I was a kid, on Sundays when all the relatives and the visiting preacher and Lord only knows how many of the church folks came home to eat with us, we had to eat in shifts. The preacher and church folks got to eat first. Then the grown-up relatives, often so many that even they had to take turns. Then, just before we thought we'd starve to death, we kids got a chance at what was left.

Until I was grown and married, I detested fried chicken because I didn't know those scrawny birds had any parts to them except feet and necks. That's one lesson I mislearned at this table.

I really am joking and not whining when I tell my grandkids that I was born in an awkward generation. During all of my growing-up days, kids like me waited while the adults filled their plates, savored bread that was still oven hot, and emptied many of the tastiest dishes. Then I got to be an adult myself and discovered that the rules had flip-flopped. Some time when I wasn't watching close enough, the Emily Posts or Martha Stewarts of the etiquette world decreed that in civilized, courteous homes, if anybody had to wait for lunch, the smallest kids should be fed first.

So all of my life, I moan in jest, I've been at the back of the line—waiting while the food vanishes. Those who hear my sad tale often have the temerity to observe that I don't appear to have missed many meals. Such cheekiness would be insulting if it were not so true.

But (and now I really am telling you the truth) this old table does conjure up memories of Sundays when my siblings and my cousins and I wiggled through seemingly endless sermons in Sunday morning church services, only to come home and wait until 2 P.M. for lunch because the same windy preacher was sitting at this table stuffing himself and telling stories that seemed to us kids to be as long—and often as pointless—as his earlier sermon. This was admittedly a childish perception.

During those memorable days I learned for the first time that empty bellies actually do growl. I grant you that's not the most important truth I ever came across, but that was the time in my life when this bit of universal insight was revealed to me.

When I got old enough to pay attention to such things, I was fascinated by the light that dangled above the center of this table. Suspended on twisted, fabric-insulated wires, the naked bulb pendulumed from the center of the kitchen ceiling.

In those early days the kitchen had no electrical outlets, so Grandmother's first electric iron had to be plugged into a tree of plastic plugs that screwed into the light socket above that one bulb. It's a wonder she didn't overload the circuit and burn the house down.

At night in those pre-air-conditioning days, I remember that suspended bulb lazily swinging to and fro when any errant but welcome breeze blew through the open windows. Meanwhile all of those who sat around this table dodged the dizzy moths and other light-obsessed bugs that kamikazied overhead. It sounds rather dismal and primitive, I know, but we thought it was great. Compared to the folks down the street who still used candles and kerosene lamps, we were grateful to have a kitchen table lit up so brightly.

This old table saw its heaviest use in the wintertime. In the southeast corner of the kitchen stood what was considered back in World War II days the modern coal-oil stove I described in an earlier chapter. On days when bitter northers plunged the mercury below freezing, our grandparents closed all the doors to the kitchen and heated this single room in a house that was already much too small to hold all the invading grandkids and their parents.

On bitterly cold days—especially during holiday times—the grown-ups nestled around this table, drinking coffee, swapping tales, while half a dozen of us rug rats swarmed around their feet or squeezed close between their shoulders, trying to get nearer to the fun and conversation going on around this table. Nobody seemed worried that we were sardined around it. Instead, everybody acted like they thought it was a special place to be.

If we had been a family that didn't like each other, I guess those winter days of enforced togetherness would have been tough to endure. If distrust and ill-concealed hostility had lurked in our links to all the in-laws and shirttail kin who surrounded this table back then, the memories I share today would be nightmares instead of warm fuzzies.

Back then—in my earliest school days—I had no way to know that people in some families yell and insult and curse one another.

In all my growing-up days I cannot recall a single angry, nasty word uttered by any member of our extended family at this table. Decades later I now know just how rare and precious a memory like that must be.

Come summertime, this same table became a home economics learning lab long before anybody dreamed of putting such a facility in a public school classroom. I'm not sure just how it got started, but back in those years when school vacations were still long enough for summers to mean something, my grandmother clustered a troupe of girls in her home at least once a week.

At this table Grandmother taught those girls how to cook and bake and sew. And, more important, she taught them to love the Lord and his word. Six decades later I still run across some of "Mrs. Key's girls," and a glow of enchantment still dances in their eyes when they recall the magical hours they spent in this room around this table. Forever it changed their lives.

How many of us have time for kids who aren't our own, kids who aren't assigned to us by some scouting office or Little League organizer, kids we don't inherit on this year's Bible class roll or in this summer's church camp? Do we think we have hours enough in our over-obligated lives to spend quality time imparting life skills and lessons of faith to youngsters whose only claim to our attention is the fact that they are "there"?

Somewhere in his vast body of writings the Scottish writer George MacDonald calls out to the church, "Brothers, have you found your king? There He is, kissing little children and saying they are like God." This is a biblical sketch of Jesus, of course—Jesus, the one who scolded his men when they scolded parents because they were trying to "bother" the Master with their brats.

Can you and I be bothered by toddlers or teens whose only glimpse of Jesus might be through our words or in our smile?

My grandmother spent innumerable hours out of her best years making sure that the girls in her little church and any of their friends who might tag along would grow up knowing the Lord she loved. She was like the psalmist who said,

> *I will open my mouth in parables,*
> *I will utter . . . things from of old—*
> > *what we have heard and known,*
> > *what our fathers have told us.*
> *We will not hide them from their children;*
> > *we will tell the next generation*
> *the praiseworthy deeds of the* LORD,
> > *his power, and the wonders he has done*
> > (Ps. 78:2–4).

Bible stories, cookie recipes, and pinafore patterns seemed to be a palatable mix when served at this table to that gaggle of girls who so adored the grandmother God gave me.

May God forgive the wretched Pharisees who decided by some strange form of theological casuistry that my grandmother's patient and loving instruction to that band of church girls and their neighborhood friends here in her own private kitchen somehow violated the eternal rules of God's kingdom.

Never mind that in Titus 2 the Scriptures plainly instruct the older women in the Christian community to teach the younger women exactly the sort of skills and information my Grandmother was imparting to "her" girls. Those spiritual pygmies dared to pontificate that my saintly grandmother would dishonor the Lord and bring reproach on his church if she told Bible stories to the neighborhood urchins or imparted domestic training to teenagers whose own mothers often gave them little or none.

With a broken heart and with tears that lasted for a decade or more, my godly, compliant grandmother acquiesced to the nonsensical mandates of those benighted church leaders, but not before she blessed "her girls" and changed their lives forever by the lessons they learned around this table.

The kitchen in my grandparents' homeplace looks a lot different now than it did back then. With modern lighting, updated kitchen cabinets, an efficient gas wall heater, and carpeted floors, Grandmother and Granddaddy wouldn't recognize it. At least not until they spotted the table. Their table. Just like it was when they sat down at it almost forty-five years ago to share an evening meal, not knowing it would be their last one in this kitchen at this table. In their mind they were only leaving the old homeplace temporarily, to live with my Aunt Vernie until their health improved.

After I bought their old home, I chose in those first months to keep it intact, the table ready at any moment to resume its accustomed role, at least until both of my grandparents had died and their hope-salvaging dream of "coming home again someday" died with them.

My well-past-retirement-age psychology professor, the late Mitchell Jones, used to smile when he told us students that his concept of hell was "where everyone is like me." He had a point, but I prefer the definition proposed by one modern novelist who wrote, "Life without hope is hell."

As long as my mother's parents were alive, I felt compelled to preserve for them the hope which most of us in the family knew to be a fiction—the hope that one day soon they would get strong enough to return to their cherished home and resume life here together.

Granddaddy had been healthy as a horse, much stronger than most of us citified grandkids, until that fateful day when the steering mechanism of his aging Ford pickup came unbuckled while he was driving to the ranch to check on his sheep. Until his old truck burrowed nose-first at sixty mph into a highway embankment and his steering wheel indented the bones in his chest, he had been able to outwork most men half his age. But his bruised heart never healed enough for him to work again.

We watched sadly as his physical health waned and Grandmother's emotional stamina dwindled, leaving them less and less able to live alone. After he died, she chose to move to the county nursing home, perched on the hill across the creek bed, with a perfect view of her own home just a city block or so away.

We assured her—and she gloried in the fact—that she could go back to that house any time she chose to. She never chose to. We didn't expect her to. But she could. And that's what mattered. As long as her thoughts were clear, she clung tenaciously to that hope.

When we lose hope, things go to pot in a hurry, don't they? Several decades ago in my town the citizens voted to build a new hospital. Just as soon as they voted to abandon the old one, which previously had been kept in good repair, it began to deteriorate before our eyes. Nobody tried anymore to patch or paint or replace worn-out equipment. Once the keepers of the building decided that it had no future, I was amazed at how quickly a solid building fell into disrepair. The same thing happens in our souls when hope is lost. That's why I thought it was worth anything it might cost me to preserve my grandmother's last shred of hope.

In her touching journal *A Circle of Quiet*, Madeleine L'Engle reminds her readers of the doomsday gloom that permeated the thinking of a whole generation during the height of the Cold War at the time of the Cuban missile crisis. She says she didn't realize just how brutally the pall of fear had oppressed even the very young until one night when her family was listening to the news. Her youngest child was at that time a second-grader. Mimicking the weather report, he announced, "Storms tomorrow." And then he added cryptically, "If there is a tomorrow" (105).

None of us lives well without a firm hope of tomorrow. Therein lies a key reason for judging the Christian faith to be superior to all others in the theological marketplace. Buddhists are taught to find happiness by teaching themselves through rigorous disciplines to extinguish all hopes. Hindus find themselves trapped in the endless cycle of repeated incarnations—most of them in ignoble life forms, and the only possible escape promised is eventual release into nirvana—into nothingness. But in Christ we vibrate with hope that one day God will finally redeem us and take us to be with him in glory.

In his *Communicator's Commentary* on Hosea, Lloyd Ogilvie expresses it well: "God believes in our future more than our past. He has plans for us." Or, as the apostle Peter put it, "We have been born anew to a living hope by the resurrection of Jesus Christ from the dead" (1 Pet. 1:3 RSV).

Tonight when I drove into town and opened up my grandparents' much-neglected homeplace to spend a few days studying and writing here, my first hour in the old house was a busy one. I swept off the front porch, dusted off the window sills, swabbed off the cabinet tops, and washed the blown-in dust and grit off the top of this table that now holds my laptop computer.

As I washed last fall's coffee stains off the table top, suddenly it hit me that the last time my brothers and I sat around this table, our father was with us. [I wrote these final words in 2000.]

We had clustered here at the old homeplace for two reasons. At least twice each year we try to spend two or three days on this property, weed-eating fence rows and battling the mesquite shoots and prickly pear irruptions that threaten to take over the place.

But last fall we also gathered here to attend to the task of burying our father's oldest sister, our dear Aunt Nola, late that week. After the funeral up in tiny O'Donnell, Texas, we drove back south to Coke County to enjoy one more precious day in this old house together.

And the last time we gathered around this table was when my father sat down at one corner of it to doctor his stove-perked coffee with the fake sugar and cream that he somehow managed to strew all over the table or cabinet top every time he prepared to drink coffee. Some of the stains I washed up tonight were the stains Dad left behind five months ago.

Almost seventy years earlier he had eaten his first meal at this table when he came to my mother's house here in the little town of Robert Lee to meet her parents and to ask for her hand in marriage. On that October morning in 1999 when we four sons drank one final cup of coffee with our father before all of us scattered toward our homes, we sat around this table and he laughed as he recalled how nervous he had been during that long-ago meal in this same room at this same table.

As Dad stirred his coffee, he told us that when he got up enough courage to broach the subject of possibly getting married to our mother, our grandfather abruptly rose from this table and, without a word, stalked out the back kitchen door toward the animal pens out back. Our father said his heart sank because he was certain he had offended his sweetheart's dad.

Later, Dad told us as he spread coffee stains all over his corner of the table top, he found out that our grandfather was not unhappy at him. He was just so attached to his oldest daughter that it broke his heart to think of her leaving home, and at first he couldn't talk about it. So Granddaddy had retreated to the pasture to get his emotions under control.

That late October Saturday when he made that familiar coffee mess turned out to be the last time our father would ever sit at this table. Three months later his heart failed. Tonight his body rests beneath the sod of the family cemetery four miles south of this place, and I sit here at this table tonight alone. Remembering.

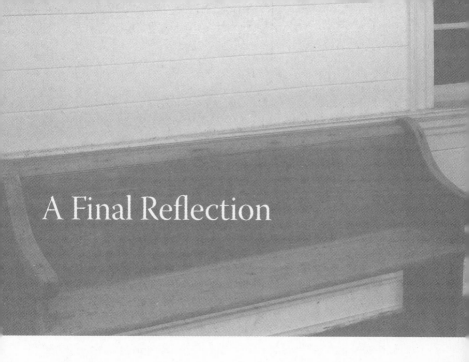

A Final Reflection

Here I am, back at the Key Place again, and my soul is once more at rest.

This morning I have been reading under the Arizona cypress tree, enjoying the shade on the west side of the house.

Spring came early this year. In early March we could have an icy norther howling in from the plains, but the morning sun today is bright and the light breeze is balmy. In my short-sleeved T-shirt I am comfortable in the shade. The cacophony of countless birds flitting through the bushes and creek cane and fence-line trees signals a springtime feeding frenzy. They seem to agree with me that it's a great day to be alive in Coke County.

I mentioned that I have been reading this morning. As I prepared to head south three days ago, one book I snatched from the growing pile on my desk was given to me by my dear friend, Dr. Dale Roller. On a recent trip he came across Newt Gingrich's *Rediscovering God in America* with its brief but interesting tour of the monuments and historic sites near the Capitol in Washington. The book focuses on the prevalence of inscriptions and quotations that reflect our nation's historic dependence on God. Typical of the book's content are Abraham Lincoln's words written in 1862 during the Civil War: "We cannot but believe that He who made the world still governs it" (54).

Having taught the academic Bible course in a public high school for forty years now, I took special note of something I had not previously heard about America's third president. Gingrich says, "When Thomas Jefferson wrote the first plan of education adopted by the District of Columbia, he used the Bible and Isaac Watts's hymnal as the principal texts for teaching reading to students" (46).

I sat under the Arizona cypress tree, pondering that line. If the man who penned much of our U.S. Constitution chose the Bible and a book of Christian hymns as the reading texts in a public school classroom, how in the name of reason could any modern judge or legislator conclude that the Constitution bans prayer or the Ten Commandments or Bible reading in public education? How did we ever allow the secularists to sell us that bill of goods?

With the noisy song of the birds ringing around me and the warmth of the morning sun seeping into my gloriously idle torso, I had leaned back in my folding chair to reflect on all of this. At that moment the southeast breeze wafted to my ears the hourly sound of the Methodist church bells. As they chimed the tune, my heart supplied the familiar words:

> *O God, our help in ages past,*
> *Our hope for years to come,*
> *Our shelter from the stormy blast,*
> *And our eternal home.*

And in my heart I said, Yes, Lord. Thank You for the confirmation that You are still running our world, even if some of us modern folks are slow to acknowledge it.